AaBbCcDdEeFfGgHhIiJjKkLlMmNn

How to Plan Your School Year

Part One .. Organizing and Scheduling My School Year

Part Two .... Seasonal Activities

Linda Holliman
Joy Evans
Editor: Bob DeWeese
Graphics: Michelle Tapola
Cover: Cheryl Kashata

Part One

Organizing and Scheduling

Think about Room Arrangement

Ask yourself questions about what you need:

- How will you arrange your student desks?

- How many center work areas can you provide?

- Do you want an open rug area to gather students together for large group discussions?

- Where will students meet for small group instructions?

- How will you arrange storage?

Welcome to Learning

Room 6

List the major work areas you want to provide:

_____   _____

_____   _____

_____   _____

_____   _____

_____   _____

Sketch your classroom. Find the arrangement that seems to fit your needs and try it out.

Room Arrangement 1

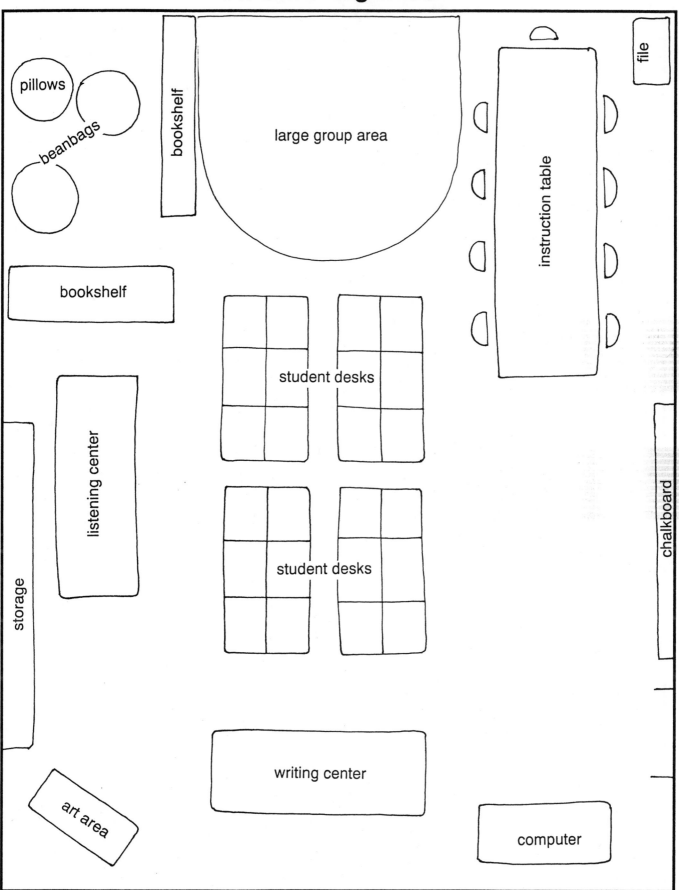

Room Arrangement 2

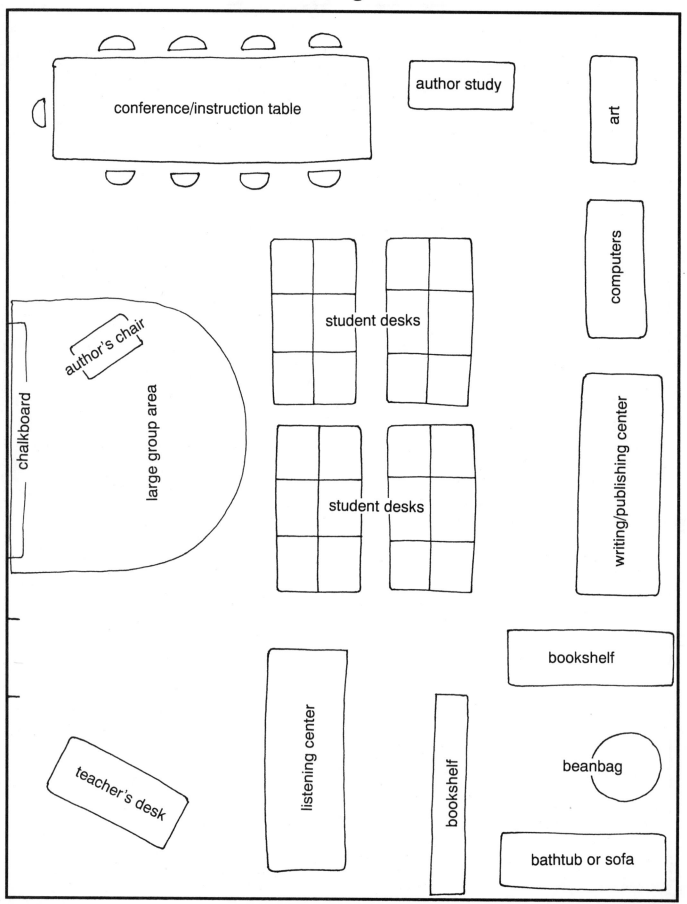

Bulletin Boards and Room Themes

What type of bulletin boards fit your teaching style?

1. A Total Room Theme
   All centers and bulletin boards can support a center theme. It could be a monthly theme or it could be a whole-year room theme.

2. Bulletin boards that reinforce skills being taught in class and also display students' work.

3. Bulletin boards constructed by students around a project topic.

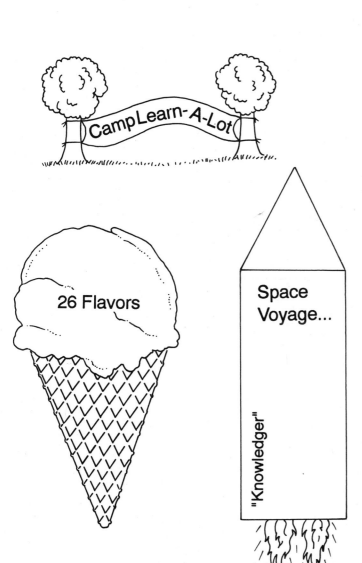

List 5 bulletin board ideas to use as great back-to-school motivators for students.

_____

_____

_____

_____

_____

_____

_____

_____

_____

_____

_____

_____

_____

_____

The Daily Schedule

Schedules vary from classroom to classroom. Let's give some thought to the schedule that will best fit your student and program needs this year. This program will include basic components but it may also leave room for some flexible planning too.

Components that many programs share:

- Opening Activities
    - Attendance Check
    - Lunch Count
    - Calendar Time
    - Daily News

- Read to Children
    - Poem
    - Newspaper
    - Books

- Writing
    - Personal Journal
    - Creative Writing
    - Nonfiction Writing

- Shared Reading Instruction
    - Three Group Rotation
    - 1. Teacher Time
    - 2. Independent Time
    - 3. Centers

- Math

- Science

- Social Studies

- Art

- Music

- Computers

What schedule do you plan to use this year?

_____

_____

_____

_____

_____

_____

_____

_____

_____

_____

_____

_____

Centers in My Classroom

Centers can be used as enrichment activities when children have finished an assignment or they can be an integral part of your curriculum. Centers can be used for exploration and discovery, or for practicing and applying skills already taught.

Keep Centers Simple!

Centers don't have to be difficult. Keep the preparation simple and have an organizational plan for moving children through them. One effective way is to set up five or more centers based on major areas of the curriculum and to maintain them, with minor changes, the rest of the year. For example...

A Writing Center

You will maintain the writing center all year, changing the "props" to reflect the unit of study or theme currently being studied in class. Provide different kinds of paper (lined, unlined, shapes, index cards), special pencils and pens, plus extras like hats or simple costumes. Provide some writing assignments which always stay up (practice handwriting, write a story, etc.), then add a few special ones to reflect the current unit or theme.

Center Organization

Keep a folder for each center and one for "future centers." Keep of copy of what you have children do at each center each week or rotation period. File these in the appropriate folders. After the first year you will have a great resource of activities from which to pull. As you find center activities you would like to try, put these in your "future" file for consideration at another time.

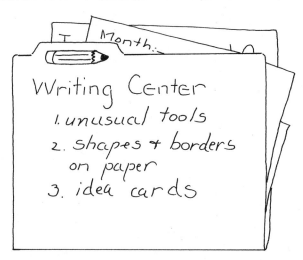

How Many Centers Do You Want?

Centers offer student-centered extensions of your regular curriculum. The number of centers you provide in your classroom depends on the space you have available and the skills that you want to reinforce.

- Listening Centers

- Read the Room Center

- Manipulative/Fine Motor Centers

- Vocabulary/Spelling

- Writing

- Science

- Social Studies/Geography

- Computer

- Math

- Library/Free Reading

- Art

- Music

- Poetry

- Box/Can

Sample Center Rotation Charts

⬤	Monday	Tuesday	Wednesday	Thursday	Friday
1	✏️	✏️	✏️	✏️	✏️
2	D	E	A	B	C
3	I	J	F	G	H
4	😊	😊	😊	😊	😊

Rabbits	Tuesday	Wednesday	Thursday	Friday	Monday	Tuesday	Wednesday	Thursday	Friday	Monday
Kenneth	1	2	3	4	5	6	7	8	9	10
Truth	10	1	2	3	4	5	6	7	8	9
Jenny	9	10	1	2	3	4	5	6	7	8
Lucas	8	9	10	1	2	3	4	5	6	7
Brian	7	8	9	10	1	2	3	4	5	6
James	6	7	8	9	10	1	2	3	4	5
Missy	5	6	7	8	9	10	1	2	3	4

How to Plan Your School Year

Center Spaces and Storage

One of the main problems with centers is space and storage.
You can overcome these problems with a little thought and creativity.

File Cabinet Center

Use the side of a file cabinet for a magnetic center. The file cabinet is already there...use it! Use this center for any skill, concept or curriculum area.   Just put magnetic tape on the back of whatever is being "manipulated."

Clipboard Centers

Clipboards also make great "centers." Hang clipboards under the chalkboard (usually wasted space).   Label the clipboards and have a can for each clipboard with activities in it for the children to use.   These activities could include manipulating, sequencing, or sorting plus some sort of format for children to use in recording what they have learned.

Cross-Legged Critters

This is one of my very favorites because these little critters stand up and contain a pocket for holding center tasks or cards. This center can be on a table or can be taken to the child's own desk for use. Once the center is no longer needed, they are simply taken apart and folded up for easy storage.

When you make cross-legged critters for a center you will want to laminate them to be long-wearing. To cross and attach the legs and the "pocket" use Velcro. You will need very little and this will not tear up the critter with repeated opening and closing.

These critter centers can be seasonal as well as thematic.

Cans, Cans, Cans

Ask the cafeteria workers to save those gallon cans for you.   Make sure all of the sharp edges have been removed.   Use spray paint to brighten up these free center containers.   Put these cans on a desk or table to hold either directions or materials needed for the center. Cans may be used over and over just by changing the contents.

Hanger Pockets

  Hanger pockets make great quick-and-easy centers.   They can be hung on a wall with activities placed inside the pocket. The child takes the materials out and works at a desk or table placed beside the hanger pocket or takes the pocket to his/her desk to work. Storage of these centers in very simple. Hang them up in your coat closet!

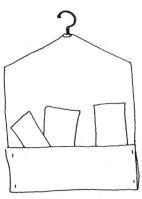

Plan for Positive Parent Communication

What is your plan for communicating with your parents this year?

1. First-month letters home are important for establishing rapport.

2. Establish a system for making and tracking notes and calls home.

3. Use a monthly NEWSLETTER to keep parents informed.

4. Plan special events for the year: Reading Party
    Parent Participation Night
    Class Plays
    Volunteer "Thank-you" Tea

List three ways you intend to establish positive parent-classroom rapport.

1. _____

2. _____

3. _____

Plan Ahead for a Substitute

**Rub a dub-dub,
Get ready for a sub!**

What might you think about ahead of time?
What could you fit into a folder in your desk labeled - "Substitute Support Folder"?

- Student names on a seating chart

- Daily schedule or an alternative sub schedule

- Lunch and attendance process

- Name tags for students

- Names to know: principal, school secretary, neighboring teachers, etc.

- Who goes where, when!

- How students get home: walking instructions, bus rules, day care situations

- Supplies

- Book projects and extensions

     How to Plan Your School Year

Welcome	Substitute Folder	Welcome

Student Names

_____ _____ _____

_____ _____ _____

_____ _____ _____

_____ _____ _____

_____ _____ _____

_____ _____ _____

_____ _____ _____

_____ _____ _____

_____ _____ W   walk
_____ _____ B   bus (include bus number)
                                      P   pick up by parent
_____ _____ DC day care

Use this area to list the special places various students go during the day.
(speech, counselor, music, ESL, other)

Who Goes?	Where?	When?
_____	_____	_____
_____	_____	_____
_____	_____	_____

Important People to Know

Principal _____   Custodian _____

Secretary _____   Other _____

Nurse _____

Lunch Schedule and Procedures

_____

_____

Daily Schedule

AM	PM

Teacher Duty Schedule: Notes:

> What time is lunch?

Books All Year Long

No matter what grade you teach or how busy your days may be, never forget that sharing literature with your students is one of the richest gifts you can give them. Plan to share all types of literature: fiction, nonfiction, poetry.

- Sometimes these books may be shared as a part of a classroom unit or theme.
- Sometimes you will share a book because it is a wonderful read-aloud selection.
- Sometimes you will read a book just because you like it.

Make a list of the titles that you **must** read a loud to your class this year.

Books to Include

Beginning Books

My Teacher Sleeps in School by Leatie Weiss; Puffin Books, 1984
The Teacher from the Black Lagoon by Mike Thaler; Scholastic, 1989
Never Spit on Your Shoes by Denys Cazet; Orchard Books, 1988
Anabelle Swift, Kindergartner by Amy Schwartz; Orchard Books, 1988
Seven Froggies Went to School by Kate Duke; Dutton, 1985
Toad School by Cathy Bellows; Macmillan, 1990
It Happens to Everyone by Bernice Myers; Lothrop, Lee and Shepard, 1990
Take Time to Relax by Nancy Carlson; Viking, 1991
Knots on a Counting Rope by Bill Martin, Jr., and John Archambault; Henry Holt, 1986
My Grandmother's Cookie Jar by Montzalee Miller; Price, Stern, Sloan, 1987
I Spent My Summer Vacation Kidnapped in Space by Martyn N. Godfrey; Apple, 1990
The Green Book by Jill Paton Walsh; Farrar, Straus, & Giroux, 1982
The Story Snail by Anne Rockwell; Aladdin Books, 1974
Amazing Grace by Mary Hoffman and Carolyn Binch; Dial Books, 1991
My Stories by Hildy Calpurina Rose by Dale Gottlieb; Knopf, 1991
Stories from the Big Chair by Ruth Wallace-Brodeur; McElderry Books, 1989
School After Dark by Peter Hannan; Knopf, 1991
Chrysanthemum by Kevin Henkes; Trumpet Books, 1991
Angry Arthur by Hiawyn Oram; Trumpet Book Club, 1982

Birthday Books

Mr. Rabbit and the Lovely Present by Charlotte Zolotow; Harper Trophy, 1962
Happy Birthday, Dear Duck by Eve Bunting; Clarion, 1988
The Birthday Moon by Lois Duncan; Penguin, 1989
Ask Mr. Bear by Marjorie Flack; Macmillan, 1932
Mary Wore Her Red Dress and Henry Wore His Green Sneakers by Merle Peek; Clarion, 1985
My Presents by Rod Campbell; Aladdin Books, 1988
Benjamin's 365 Birthdays by Judi Barrett; Antheneum, 1974

Book Projects

The Arrow by Alex Brychta
Just Like Everyone Else by Karla Kushkin
Pickle Things by Marc Brown
The Mysteries of Harris Burdick by Chris Van Allsburg
Christina Katerina and the Box by Patricia Lee Gauch
Old Black Fly by Jim Aylesworth

The Big Orange Splot by Daniel Manus Pinkwater
12 Ways to Get to 11 by Eve Merriam
Fortunately by Remy Charlip
It Looked Like Spilt Milk by Charles G. Shaw
Wilfrid Gordon McDonald Partridge by Mem Fox
Brown Bear, Brown Bear by Bill Martin, Jr.
Somewhere Today by Bert Kitchen
Hiawatha by Henry Wadsworth Longfellow
The Moon by Robert Louis Stevenson
The Boy with Square Eyes by Juliet and Charles Snape
The Wretched Stone by Chris Van Allsburg
The Magic Box by Barbara Brenner
Messages in the Mailbox: How to Write a Letter
by Loreen Leedy
Dear Mr. Blueberry by Simon James
Kate Heads West by Pat Brisson
Kate on the Coast by Pat Brisson
Your Best Friend, Kate by Pat Brisson
The Snake's Mistake by Keith Faulkner
Crictor by Tomi Ungerer
Once Upon A to Z by Jody Linscott
Alligators All Around by Maurice Sendak

A Book Project Form

Book: Frog and Toad Are Friends
Frog and Toad Together
By: Arnold Lobel

Extension Activity and Materials:

Frog Cross-legged Critters
I need green and brown 9x12 construction paper.
Also: white paper, glue, stapler

Curriculum Connections:

Math
Buttons — sorting
(co-op groups — each group
sets own criteria)

Science
Frog/Toad — compare.
Guided report form for
gathering info. Life Cycle

Social Studies
Friendship — What
makes a good friend

Writing
Write a new frog
and toad story. Frog and Toad
on an adventure. ⟨Beg⟩
⟨End⟩ Frog and Toad
are friends.

Art
Paper Plate Frogs
Need: 1 plate per child,
green const. paper, white
paper, red scraps. Crayon

© 1994 by Evan-Moor Corp.   20   How to Plan Your School Year

---

Book Projects I want to develop:

_____

_____

_____

_____

_____

_____

_____

A Book Project Form

Book:

_____

By: _____

Extension Activity and Materials:

_____

_____

_____

Curriculum Connections:

Math

_____

_____

_____

Social Studies

_____

_____

_____

Art

_____

_____

_____

Science

_____

_____

_____

Writing

_____

_____

_____

The First Week of School

• Let's learn about each other and get acquainted. What activities and projects would be fun to share that encourage interaction and sharing?

• We also want to take advantage of this new beginning to set up classroom procedures and establish rules and standards.

• Now would be an ideal time to encourage oral and written activities about what everyone did over the vacation break.

Books about Getting Acquainted:

We Are Best Friends by Aliki; Greenwillow, 1982

Will I Have a Friend? by Miriam Cohen; Macmillan, 1987

Timothy Goes To School by Rosemary Wells; Dial, 1981

Crow Boy by Taro Yashima; Viking, 1955

The Empty Schoolhouse by Natalie Savage Carlson; Harper, 1965

The World's Greatest Expert on Absolutely Everything is Crying by Barbara Battner; Harper, 1984

Nothing's Fair in Fifth Grade by Barthe DeClements; Viking, 1981

Yellow Fur and Little Hawk by Wilma Pitchford; Putnam, 1980

Rosie and Michael by Judith Viorst; Atheneum, 1974

Do Bananas Chew Gum? by Jamie Gilson; Lothrop, 1980

My Friend Leslie: The Story of a Handicapped Child by George Ancona; Lothrop, 1983

I'm the Best by Marjorie Weinman Sharmat; Holiday House, 1991

Be a Detective

Find a person that can answer "yes" to the question.
Have that person sign his/her name on the line.

1. Do you have a baby sister? _____

2. Do you have a pet bird? _____

3. Have you ever been to Disney World? _____

4. Have you ever flown on a plane? _____

5. Can you tap dance? _____

6. Can you speak a language other than English? _____

7. Do you know how to swim? _____

8. Did you go to a different school last year? _____

9. Did you have a birthday during the summer? _____

10. Do you have blue eyes? _____

11. Can you ride a horse? _____

12. Can you whistle? _____

13. Are you left-handed? _____

14. Have you ever tasted sushi? _____

15. Were you born in California? _____

     How to Plan Your School Year

My Summer Vacation

Where did you go during summer vacation?

- Read *Stringbean's Trip to the Shining Sea* by Vera & Jennifer Williams (Greenwillow, 1988). Discuss Stringbean's journey. Use this as a starting point in discussing vacation trips (short & long) taken by your students.

  Where did you go?
  Who went along?
  How did you travel?
  What exciting adventures happened on your trip?
  Describe the best/worst day of your journey.

- Get a large map. Have students locate the places they visited on their trips. Invite students to share postcards they have received from friends.

- Design original postcards and write a message to a friend. Tell about one thing you did during the summer.

- Create individual accordion books to illustrate trips students have taken.

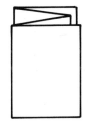

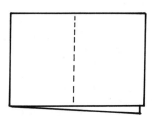

Day 1 — Discuss trips. Have your students fold the accordion and design the cover.
Day 2 — Decide what events will be illustrated. Begin the first illustration. Write two or more sentences at the bottom of the page. Do as many pages as you have time for.
Day 3 — Continue the illustrations and short paragraphs.

NOTE: Another good book to motivate a discussion of summer trips is *Three Days on a River in a Red Canoe* by Vera B. Williams; Greenwillow, 1986.

 How to Plan Your School Year

Did your relatives visit you during the summer?

- Read *The Relatives Came* by Cynthia Rylant (Bradbury Press, 1985).
  Discuss the events that occurred when the relatives arrived.
  Then discuss what has happened to your students when their
  own relatives have come for a visit.

  Why did they come?
  How long did they stay?
  How did the visit change how things are done in your home?
  What was the best part of the visit?
  What was the worst part of the visit?

- Have students illustrate a scene from a visit by relatives.

I just stayed home all summer.

- Discuss and list types of home activities students might have participated in during
  the summer.

  What are ways to have fun in our town during the summer?

  What did you do with your friends?

  What did you do with your family?

  What did you do when you were by yourself?

  Did you do something you thought would be great fun that
  turned out to be a disaster?

  Did you do something because your parents made you that
  turned out to be fun?

- Mark on a community map all the places students spent time during the summer.
  Tally the number of students that went to each of these spots and make a graph.

- Make a time line of summer activities.

My
Master Planning Calendar

*I am organized!
What month is this?*

HONEY

Use these pages to help you organize your school year. The calendar pages have been designed so that you can remove them and use them in your classroom.

You may choose to use these pages several different ways:

- You might 3-hole punch the calendar pages and keep them together in a binder.

- You may tape each month's calendar to a folder, then collect work pages and activities inside the folder for that month.

- You may know a better way of doing this!

How to Make the Calendar Work for You

1. Outline the specific skills you need to teach this year on the skill pages for each curriculum area.

2. Do a general plan of the units you want to include in this school year. Plug these units into the calendar in the month which you will teach them.

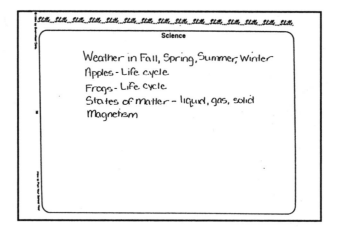

3. Mark all dates on this calendar that affect your program.

- Parent-Teacher Conferences
- Vacations
- Field Trips
- Guest Speakers

Use the calendar as a planning device. It can serve you well.

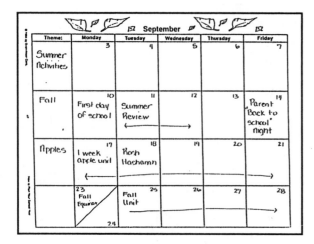
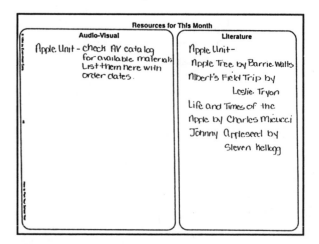

Use the back of each calendar to keep track of specific resources you have found useful that month. Next year's planning will be a snap with all of this organized for you.

Language Arts

Social Studies

Math

29

Science

Resources for This Month

Literature

Audio-Visual

October

Theme:	Monday	Tuesday	Wednesday	Thursday	Friday

Resources for This Month

Literature

Audio-Visual

November

Theme:	Monday	Tuesday	Wednesday	Thursday	Friday

Resources for This Month

Literature

Audio-Visual

December

Theme:	Monday	Tuesday	Wednesday	Thursday	Friday

Resources for This Month

Literature

Audio-Visual

January

Theme:	Monday	Tuesday	Wednesday	Thursday	Friday

Resources for This Month

Literature

Audio-Visual

February

Theme:	Monday	Tuesday	Wednesday	Thursday	Friday

Resources for This Month

Literature

Audio-Visual

March

Theme:	Monday	Tuesday	Wednesday	Thursday	Friday

Resources for This Month

Literature

Audio-Visual

April

Theme:	Monday	Tuesday	Wednesday	Thursday	Friday

Resources for This Month

Literature

Audio-Visual

How to Plan Your School Year

May

Theme:	Monday	Tuesday	Wednesday	Thursday	Friday

September

Theme:	Monday	Tuesday	Wednesday	Thursday	Friday

Resources for This Month

Literature

Audio-Visual

June

Theme:	Monday	Tuesday	Wednesday	Thursday	Friday

Resources for This Month

Literature

Audio-Visual

How to Plan Your School Year

July

Theme:	Monday	Tuesday	Wednesday	Thursday	Friday

Resources for This Month

Literature

Audio-Visual

August

Theme:	Monday	Tuesday	Wednesday	Thursday	Friday

Resources for This Month

Literature

Audio-Visual

How to Plan Your School Year

Part Two

Seasonal Activities

Develop Celebrations of Your Own

Read *I'm in Charge of Celebrations* (Byrd Baylor; Charles Scribner & Sons, 1986) to stimulate a class discussion.

You might ask questions such as:

Why do people celebrate certain events or experiences?

What events are celebrated by your family?

Is the event celebrated by many people or is it celebrated only by your family?

Can you remember something special that has happened to you that you would like to celebrate?

How might you celebrate the experience?

What has happened in our class this year that is worthy of a special celebration?

What can we do to celebrate this experience?

Create celebrations around the special events that happen in class (something seen or done on a field trip, successfully completing a book or learning a new skill, eggs hatching or seeds sprouting, an unexpected event, a special visitor, etc.).

Help your students create a class book (or individual books) about the celebrations in their lives.

Let's Celebrate
by Caroline Parry;
Kids Can, 1987
This book is a good
source of information
about Canadian holidays.

Celebrate Fall

Facts about Fall:

• Northern Hemisphere - The approximate months of fall are September, October, and November.

• Fall Equinox - September 23
The sun is over the equator. This causes days and nights of equal lengths in the Northern and Southern Hemispheres.

• When the length of the light and dark changes, it causes trees to drop leaves and become dormant.

• Some animals hibernate, some migrating animals head south, and some bury food.

• Crops are harvested before the snow comes.

How to Plan Your School Year

Poems for Fall

Share books and poems about fall with your students.

The boughs do shake and the bells do ring
So merrily comes our harvest in,
Our harvest in, our harvest in,
So merrily comes our harvest in.
We've ploughed, we've sowed,
We've reaped, we've mowed,
We've got our harvest in.

Anonymous

When all the leaves are off the boughs,
    And nuts and apples gathered in,
And cornstalks waiting for the cows,
    And pumpkins safe in barn and bin;
Then Mother says: "My children dear,
    The fields are brown, and Autumn flies;
Thanksgiving Day is very near,
    And we must make Thanksgiving pies!"

Anonymous

Five little squirrels
Sat in a tree,
The first one said,
"What do I see?"
The second one said,
"A man with a gun."
The third one said,
"We'd better run."
The fourth one said,
"Let's hide in the shade."
The fifth one said,
"I'm not afraid."
Then BANG went the gun,
And how they did run!

Unknown

The Oak Tree by Paula Hogan; Raintree, 1979
Autumn Story by Jill Barklem; Putnam's Sons, 1980
Merrily Comes Our Harvest In by Lee Bennett Hopkins; Harcourt, 1978
Marmalade's Yellow Leaf by Cindy Wheeler; Knopf, 1982
Autumn by Louis Santrey; Troll, 1983

 How to Plan Your School Year

Note: This page is from EMC 225 *Write Every Day*

Write About Fall

Story Starters

1. The best thing about fall is...
2. The worst thing about fall is...
3. Pretend you are a leaf on a tall tree. Describe what happens to you when autumn comes. Tell how you change and how you feel.
4. Think of some interesting ways to use the colorful fall leaves.
5. It is fall in the woods. You are a little squirrel. How would you get ready for the coming winter?
6. Imagine you are rolling around in a pile of autumn leaves. Describe what you smell, hear, and touch. Use words that make me feel like I am there too.
7. Describe your feelings when you hear the first school bell in September.
8. Dad raked the backyard this morning. There is a huge pile of leaves just sitting there. I think I will...
9. It is so cold you can see your breath. Describe how you will get ready to go outside.
10. One crisp fall morning I decided to take a stroll in the woods. I had no way of knowing that...

Titles

1. How Fall Got Its Name
2. Fall Colors
3. How to Climb a Tree
4. Why Leaves Change Their Colors (invent a legend)
5. One Cold, Frosty Morning
6. An Unusual Day at School
7. The Hardest Part of School this Year
8. The Year the Leaves Turned Purple
9. Jack Frost
10. In the Squirrel's Nest

Activities for September

Other celebrations to plan this month:

September 18 - Rosh Hashanah

September 20 - Ice Cream Cone's Birthday

September 22 - Happy Birthday Fall

September 23 - Native American Day

September 28 - Yom Kippur

National Dog Week

Monarch Butterfly Migration

Authors' September Birthdays:

September 2 - Bernard Most	*If the Dinosaurs Came Back*
September 5 - Paul Fleischman	*Joyful Noises: Poems for Two Voices*
September 8 - Jack Prelutsky	*Something Big Has Been Here*
September 14 - Elizabeth Winthrop	*Shoes*
September 15 - Tomie de Paola	*Strega Nona*
September 15 - Robert McCloskey	*Make Way for Ducklings*

Celebrate Johnny Appleseed's birthday on
September 26 by beginning a unit on apples.
How many different apples are there?

**Apples
Apples
Apples**

 Develop the beginnings of a unit about apples by reading:

Apple Tree by Barrie Watts; Silver Burdett Press, 1986
The Seasons of Arnold's Apple Tree by Gail Gibbons; Harcourt
Brace Jovanovich, 1984
Apple Pigs by Ruth Orbach; Collins World, 1977
Johnny Appleseed by Steven Kellogg; Morrow Junior Books, 1988
Albert's Field Trip by Leslie Tryon
The Life and Times of the Apple by Charles Micucci
How to Eat Fried Worms by Thomas Rockwell

 Sequence the steps in the development of an apple. (See page 63.)

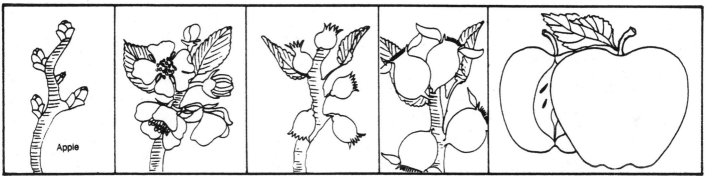

Apple

 Plant apple seeds and watch them sprout.

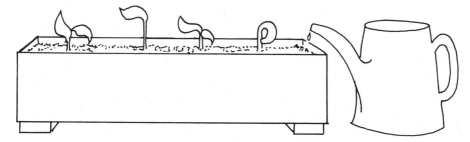

 Make applesauce, candied apples, apple cake. Have every child
in your class bring his or her favorite apple recipe. Compile all the
recipes into a class cookbook and have an apple recipe tasting day.
All the recipes from the cookbook are prepared by the family
apple "chef" and brought to school for an afternoon of culinary delight.

An Apple Activity

The subject of apples can lead into great lessons on descriptive words and categories. Have a sampling of apple varieties on hand for the class to nibble as they brainstorm about apples. Develop these categories during class discussion. Then follow up by writing about apples.

Look! Feel! Taste!

Taste and Texture
1. sweet
2. crunchy
3. juicy

Parts
1. skin
2. pulp
3. core
4. seeds

Ways to Use
1. juice
2. pie
3. sauce
4. fritters

Names
1. Jonathan
2. Red Delicious
3. Winesap
4. McIntosh
5. Gravenstein

Look
1. red, green, yellow
2. big and round
3. smooth skin

A Special Shape Book!

- red construction paper
- green construction paper
- writing paper

This double-folded shape book is a great starting point for a story about who took a bite out of the apple.

  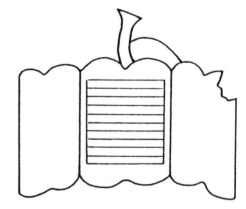

Use the vocabulary developed in the lesson above to create super sentences about juicy apples.

Tommy picked up a big, round, red apple.
I bit into the sweet, crunchy apple Mother put in my lunch.
A spicy smell filled the kitchen when the apple pie began to cook.
A large, brown worm began to crawl out of the apple's tasty core.

Apple Life Cycle

Give each child a 4" x 6" file card with two slits already cut.
Child cuts out the pictures and pastes them in the correct order on the "pull" strip.
Thread the strip through the card. Pull to watch the apple grow.

1 Color

2 Cut

3 Paste

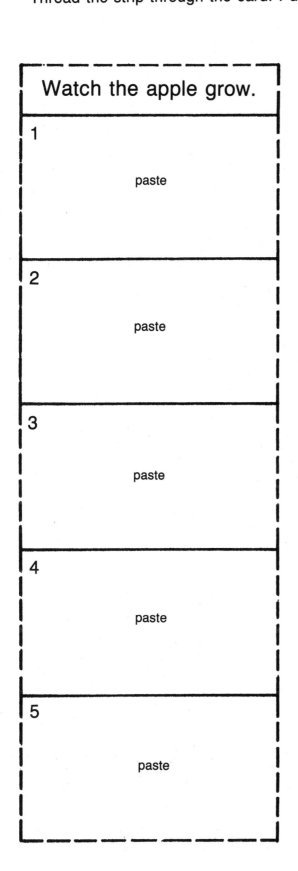

Apple Art

Make these apple cut-out pictures and display them as a border across your bulletin board.

Add a caption such as:

> You are the apple of my eye!
>
> What tasty work is here.
>
> The Pick of the Crop

This lesson is a natural accompaniment to a unit on various types of apples. These are colorful when used alone, but may also be assembled on a bulletin board for a striking effect.

Materials:

Black construction paper squares
Red, green or yellow squares (slightly smaller than the black)
White squares (smaller than the other colors)
Scraps of brown (stem) and green (leaf)
Scissors, paste, black crayon

3. Paste the white shape on the colored shape. Use black crayon to add seeds.

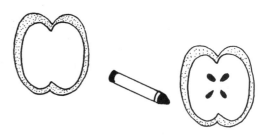

Steps to follow:

1. Fold red, yellow or green paper in half. Cut on the fold.

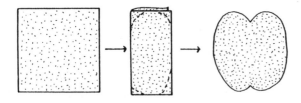

2. Fold and cut the white paper.

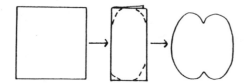

4. Cut a stem from brown and a leaf from green.

5. Arrange all of the pieces on the black square. Paste the pieces in place.

How to Plan Your School Year

Happy Birthday Fall!

Celebrate the beginnng of fall with a birthday party in its honor!

• Provide giant sugar cookies for the children to decorate using fall colors.

• Make leaves out of orange, red, yellow and brown construction paper by having children trace around their hands. Use these "leaves" for bulletin board borders, fall trees in the hallway or in a fall collage. Move into a science lesson on why leaves change colors.

Grandparents' Day
(the first Sunday after Labor Day)

Kevin's Grandma by Barbara Williams; E.P. Dutton, 1975
I Dance in My Red Pajamas by Edith Thatcher Hurd; Harper & Row, 1982
When I Was Young in the Mountains by Cynthia Rylant; E.P. Dutton, 1982
Nana Upstairs & Nana Downstairs by Tomie de Paola; G.P. Putnam's Sons, 1973
The Two of Them by Aliki; Greenwillow Books, 1979
Good As New by Barbara Douglass; Lothrop, Lee & Shepard, 1982
Through Grandpa's Eyes by Patricia MacLachlan; Harper & Row, 1980
My Grandson Lew by Charlotte Zolotow; Harper & Row, 1974
Annie and the Old One by Miska Miles; Little, Brown & Co., 1971
After the Goat Man by Betsy Byars; The Viking Press, 1974
The Magic Grandfather by Jay Williams; Four Winds Press, 1979
The Patchwork Quilt by Valerie Flournoy; E.P. Dutton, 1985
Grandma's Promise by Elaine Moore; Lothrop, Lee & Shepard, 1982
Knots on a Counting Rope by Bill Martin, Jr., & John Archambault; Henry Holt & Company, 1987
When Grandfather Journeys Into Winter by Craig Kee Strete; Greenwillow, 1979
Grandma's Baseball by Gavin Curtis; Crown, 1990
The Wednesday Surprise by Eve Bunting; Clarion, 1989
A Time for Remembering by Chuck Thurman; Simon and Schuster, 1989

Read *The Patchwork Quilt* by Valerie Flournoy (E.P. Dutton, 1985), *The Remembering Box* by Eth Clifford (Houghton Mifflin, 1985), and *My Grandmother's Cookie Jar* by Montzalee Miller (Price Stern Sloan, Inc., 1987).

Discuss how each of these items serves as a reminder of events from the past. Ask children to describe an object they have that reminds them of their own pasts. (You may need to have some examples ready to help them get started.) Have a quilt sharing day. Invite children and their parents to bring family quilts to class. Allow time for sharing where the quilt came from, who made it, and any history the quilt might possess. (It is especially nice if the person who made the quilt can come to tell about it.)

Create a class "remembering" box. Place objects representing class experiences in a box throughout the school year. Periodically take items out to recall the activity and how the class felt about the experience. (You might include items such as art activities, original writings, objects from field trips, or photos of class members and visitors.)

Share "Grandparent" Memories

- Invite grandparents to come to class to tell a story about some event from their own life (select a topic appropriate to your grade level). Grandparents who live too far away can be invited to write a story or to send a tape-recorded tale.

- Have your students write their own favorite memories about their grandparents. Display these stories on a bulletin board or bind them into a class book.

- Have a sharing time to discuss grandparents, allowing ample time for each child who wishes to tell a story about one grandparent.

- Do a letter–writing unit especially for grandparents.

- Create a "Grandparent Newsletter" to share with families.

- Make a special greeting card for Grandparents' Day.

- Have children interview one of their grandparents and write down their answers to questions such as:

  > Where and when were you born?
  >
  > What did you do for fun when you were my age?
  >
  > What was your favorite book?
  >
  > Did you ever get into trouble when you were my age?
  >
  > How did your parents punish you?
  >
  > Tell me about the place where you grew up. Was it very different than it is today? How?
  >
  > How did you meet grandmother/grandfather?
  >
  > What was my mother/father like when she/he was small?

- Encourage "Grandparent Visitations" to share memories or have a sharing time dedicated to telling favorite stories about grandparents.

The Grandparent Gazette

Issue _____   Date _____

Activities for
October

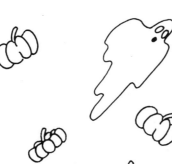

Other celebrations to plan this month:

October 15 - World Poetry Day
October 21 - Whale Watching Day
October 23 - Swallows leave San Juan Capistrano
Pasta Week
World Series Week

Authors' September Birthdays:

October 7 - Susan Jeffers   *Hiawatha*
October 21 - Janet Ahlberg   *The Jolly Postman*
October 26 - Steven Kellogg   *The Island of the Skog*

Popcorn Month

Keep them "popping" until the end of the month with a popcorn celebration.

The Popcorn Book by Tomie de Paola
Popcorn by Frank Asch
Science Fun with Peanuts and Popcorn by Rose Wyler

Use popcorn as a topic for teaching math skills in your classroom.

• Teach Tens and Ones
The popped kernals represent tens and the unpopped kernels represent the ones. Give children a "mat" to work on and have them manipulate the popcorn to represent numbers as they practice large numbers.

• Teach Estimation (See page 71.)

• Create Word Problems (See page 71.)

Use information from *The Popcorn Book* by Tomie de Paola to create a time line. Popcorn has been around for thousands of years!

Popcorn

Popcorn left in cave homes of early man.	Native Americans pop it over a fire.	We eat it from the microwave.
Prehistoric (long ago)		Today

Popcorn Math

1. Weigh the kernels before popping. Record the weight. Weigh the kernels after popping. Record the weight. Compare the two weights. Are they different? Why or why not?

2. Estimate how many cups of popped corn you will get from one cup of unpopped kernels. Record your estimate. Pop the corn. Measure the number of cups. How close was your estimate? Will you always get the same number of cups of popped corn from one cup of unpopped corn? Repeat the experiment several times and observe the results.

3. Write word problems about popcorn. (Have your students help create problems for their classmates to answer.) Adjust the difficulty of the problems to the age and ability of your students. Here are some examples to get you started.

If each child in the room gets one cup of popcorn, how many cups do we need to pop for our class?

One bag of popcorn costs $1.97. How much will six bags cost?

Mark had 88 cents, Tonya had 69 cents, and Lee had 97 cents. If they put their money together can they buy a large box of popcorn that costs $2.50? Will they get any change back?

Six friends came to Meg's slumber party. She plans to make popcorn balls. How many will she have to make so each child may have two?

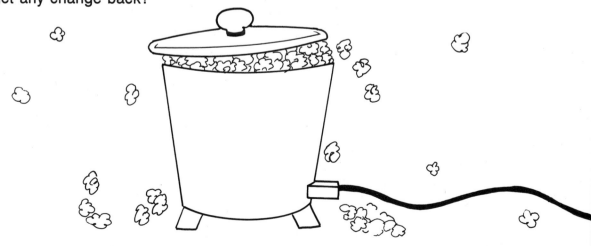

Columbus Day

October 12

In 1400 and 92
     Columbus sailed the ocean blue.
In three small ships
     That storm winds blew,
He found our land
     When it was new.

(Author unknown)

When you study Columbus and the discovery of the Americas, look at another point of view. Jane Yolen's book *Encounter* is written from the Native American viewpoint.

Christopher Columbus by Lisl Weil; Antheneum, 1983
Christopher Columbus by Gian Paolo Ceserani; Random House, 1979
I, Columbus: My Journal 1492-3 by Peter and Connie Roop, Editors; Walker, 1990
A Picture Book of Christopher Columbus by David Adler; Holiday House, 1991
Where Do You Think You're Going, Christopher Columbus? by Jean Fritz, Putnam, 1980
The Discovery of the Americas by Betsy and Giulio Maestro

Think About It:

What would have happened if Columbus had not sailed to America?

Is Indian a correct name for the people living in the Americas when Columbus arrived? Why or why not?

Who are the great explorers in modern times?

Would you have been willing to go off across an unknown sea in a small, wooden boat to search for a new land? Why or why not?

Christopher Columbus

Christopher Columbus was born in Genoa on the northern coast of Italy in 1451. The son of a master weaver, Columbus showed no interest in following in the family trade. He wanted to be a sailor! He spent his free time on the docks listening to sailors' tales of the danger and scary creatures that were to be met in the "Sea of Darkness." Columbus wanted adventure. He read the books of Marco Polo, an adventurer who had traveled overland to India, China, and Japan. He studied maps and learned how to make them.

When he was older, Columbus went to sea many times. Once an enemy attacked the ship he was on. The ship sank, but Columbus managed to get to shore. He found himself in Portugal. The year was 1476. Columbus stayed in Portugal, married, and had a son.

At this time in history, many countries were looking for a fast ocean route to the Indies, where silks, spices, and other valuable trade items could be acquired. Columbus believed that sailing west would be shorter. He also believed that God meant him to take the Christian religion across the sea and convert people to Christianity.

In 1484, at age 33, Columbus tried to convince King John of Portugal to finance a voyage. When King John said no, Columbus went to Spain to ask King Ferdinand and Queen Isabella. As Spain was involved in a war, Columbus had to wait a number of years to even see the monarchs. So certain was Columbus of finding a new route to the Indies and vast riches, that he demanded to be made governor of all the lands he discovered and to receive one-tenth of the treasures he brought back. Columbus must have been very convincing because the Spanish rulers granted him the necessary funds to make his voyage.

On August 3, 1492, the Niña, the Pinta, and the Santa Maria, loaded with 100 men, cats to catch the ships' rats, food, water, weapons, and trinkets to trade, sailed west into the open sea.

Columbus expected to reach Japan in 2400 miles. The sailors became angry and worried as it became obvious they had sailed considerably farther than that. They begged him to turn back, and even threatened to mutiny, but Columbus was able to calm their fears and convince them to go on.

On October 12, 1492, land was reached. Columbus named the land San Salvador and called the natives Indians. (He believed he'd reached the East Indies.) Searching for gold, Columbus sailed from island to island. There were many curiosities — barkless dogs, brightly-colored parrots, tobacco — but little gold. They landed on Cuba and Haiti (which Columbus named Hispaniola).

Sailing along the coast of Haiti at night, the Santa Maria ran aground. The natives they encountered had much gold. Columbus was excited. This was what they'd been searching for! He left 39 men in Hispaniola to build a fort. He sailed back to Spain for more ships to carry all the gold that would be collected by the time he returned.

On his second voyage from Spain, Columbus had 17 ships, which carried many men to settle Hispaniola and collect gold. Arriving in Hispaniola, he found that things had gone badly in his absence. The men were dead and the fort destroyed. Things went badly for the new settlers also. There was much sickness, and collecting gold was very difficult.

In 1496, Columbus again returned to Spain to attempt to explain to Ferdinand and Isabella what had gone wrong. Luckily for Columbus, the King and Queen were willing to give him another chance. This time he was sent further south in an attempt to find gold. On this voyage Columbus landed on an island, which he named Trinidad, off the coast of South America.

Arriving next in Hispaniola, Columbus discovered that the settlers were extremely unhappy. In fact they complained so loudly to Spain that Ferdinand and Isabella sent a special representative to find out what was going on. The representative arrested Columbus and sent him back to Spain in chains.

Amazingly enough, the King and Queen were willing to give Columbus one final chance. In 1502 he set sail for India again. This time he sailed up and down the coast of Central America, finding unfriendly natives and no gold. He lost two of his four ships and had to run the last two ashore on Jamaica because they were falling apart. Stranded on Jamaica for one year, Columbus did not get back to Spain until November, 1504.

Columbus died May 20, 1506, still insisting he'd found the Indies. He hadn't of course, but his four voyages started a wave of exploration which changed the course of world history.

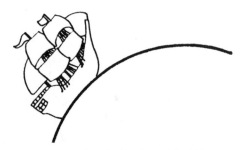

NOTE: Explorers and early immigrants make interesting topics for beginning report writing. This format is from EMC 221 *Guided Report Writing.*

Steps for a Guided Report on Christopher Columbus

Advance Preparation:

1. Gather your information.
2. Fill in the note-taking chart.
   Do this as a group.

	(Childhood) Subtopic 1	(First Voyage) Subtopic 2	(Discoveries) Subtopic 3	(Final Years) Subtopic 4
Source A				
Source B				

Steps to Follow:

1. Formulate subtopics.
   What do we want to know?

2. Research in one source.

3. Take notes on the chart.

4. Use additional sources of information.
   encyclopedia
   nonfiction books
   biographical dictionary
   magazines
   films

5. Convert notes into finished form.

6. Proofread.

7. Re-copy report in finished form.

8. Develop bibliography and title pages.

Bibliography
1. _____
2. _____
3. _____

Columbus' First Voyage

Name _____

Draw the route of Christopher Columbus' first voyage to the New World in 1492. Follow the directions below the map.

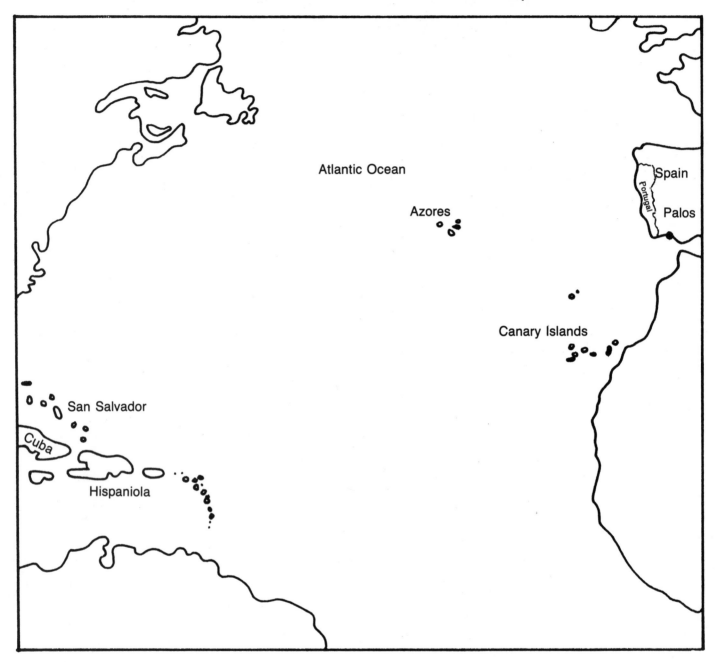

1. From Palos, Spain, sail southwest (SW) to the Canary Islands.

2. Sail west to the island of San Salvador.

3. Sail south to Cuba.

4. Sail east to Hispaniola.

5. Sail northeast (NE) toward the Azores.

6. Pass the Azores on the south and sail east to Spain.

7. Finally, sail south along the coast of Spain to Palos.

Note: This activity is from EMC 221 *Guided Report Writing.*

     How to Plan Your School Year

Outline in black.

The Santa Maria

- 9'' X 12'' white paper
- tongue depressor

1. Color the blue sea on the bottom of the paper.

2. Cut a slit at the water line.

3. Paste the sail and ship to the tongue depressor.

4. Place the ship through the slit and take the Santa Maria on its journey.

Santa Maria

Color brown.

Outline in black.

Draw Columbus' Ship

Follow these drawing steps:

Draw the water line.
Add the basic ship shape.

Add the masts.
Put on a railing and portholes.

Draw the sails full of wind.

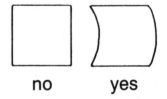

no   yes

Add the final touches.
  flags
  lines
  crow's-nest
Create a background for your
ship.

                   How to Plan Your School Year

Halloween

From Ghoulies and Ghosties,
Long-legged Beasties,
And things
That go BUMP in the night,
Good Lord, deliver us!

(Unknown)

In a dark, dark wood, there was a dark, dark house,
And in that dark, dark house, there was a dark, dark room,
And in that dark, dark room, there was a dark, dark cupboard,
And in that dark, dark cupboard, there was a dark, dark shelf,
And in that dark, dark shelf, there was a dark, dark box,
And in that dark, dark box, there was a dark, dark GHOST!

(Unknown)

Books for Halloween:

The Trouble With Mom by Babette Cole; Coward-McCann, 1983
Bony-Legs by Joanna Cole; Macmillan Publishing, 1983
Witch Lady by Nancy Carlson; Carolrhoda Books, 1985
Bunnicula by Deborah & James Howe; Atheneum, 1979
What's Happened to Harry? by Barbara Dillon; William Morrow, 1982
The Half-a-Moon Inn by Paul Fleischman; Harper & Row, 1980
Witches, Pumpkins, and Grinning Ghosts by Edna Barth; Clarion Books, 1972
The Night of the Paper Bag Monsters by Helen Craig; Alfred A. Knopf, 1985
Pumpkin Pumpkin by Jeanne Titherington; Greenwillow, 1986
The Halloween Pumpkin Smasher by Judith St. George; G. P. Putnam's Sons, 1978
The Little Old Lady Who Wasn't Afraid of Anything by Linda Williams; Thomas Y. Crowell, 1986
A Dark, Dark Tale by Ruth Brown; Dial Books for Young Readers, 1981
The Magic Pumpkin by Bill Martin, Jr., & John Archambault; Henry Holt and Company, 1989
It's Halloween by Jack Prelutsky; Greenwillow, 1977
Ghost's Hour, Spook's Hour by Eve Bunting; Clarion, 1987
Ghosts and Goosebumps selected by Bobbi Katz
Skeletons! Skeletons! All About Bones by Katy Hall
Harriet's Halloween Candy by Nancy Carlson

Let's Write about Halloween:

Story Starters for Halloween
• It was the weirdest costume I had ever seen...
• Not all monsters are scary. Igor only wanted to...
• The door opened slowly and in crept...
• I don't believe in ghosts, but that Halloween night...
• Jamie didn't enjoy being a frog. How could she
  convince the angry witch to remove the spell?...

Titles for Creative Writing
• The Sounds of Halloween
• How to Trick a Goblin
• The Littlest Jack-o'-lantern
• Flying Through Space on a Witch's Broom

Write Super Sentences for Halloween

| That witch did fly. |
| A ghost disappeared. |
| Many bats flew. |
| The skeleton rattled. |
| Some monsters groaned. |

THAT WITCH DID FLY.

1. Brainstorm — Fill in one category at a time beginning with describing words. List the children's suggestions on the chalkboard or on a chart.
2. Oral Sentences — Allow time for children to create many oral sentences using the words and phrases written on the board.
3. Write — Have the children follow the same steps to complete their own written sentences.
4. Proof and correct.

	describing words	who or what?	did what?	where?	when?
That		witch	did fly.		

Add these words and phrases to increase vocabulary and to develop new concepts.

describing words
1. bony
2. cranky
3. messy
4. rude
5. sneaky

who or what?
1. wizard
2. warlock
3. imp

did what?
1. cast a spell
2. circled on her broom
3. spilled her magic brew
4. silently crept
5. cackled wildly

when?
1. late one winter night
2. just before sunrise
3. while filling the pot
4. the night before Halloween
5. just now

where?
1. over the village
2. above the rooftops
3. on the cottage floor
4. through the dark woods
5. as she flew by

Paper Bag Monsters

Read The Night of the Paper Bag Monsters by Helen Craig (Alfred Knopf, 1985) and then create these wonderful paper bag masks. Each student may make his or her own lunch bag version or your students may cooperate in making a larger grocery bag version to enliven a bulletin board.

This mask is made from construction paper triangles all decorated with warm colors — red, orange, pink, and yellow.

This mask is made from curly strips of construction paper. Use only cool colors — green, blue, and purple.

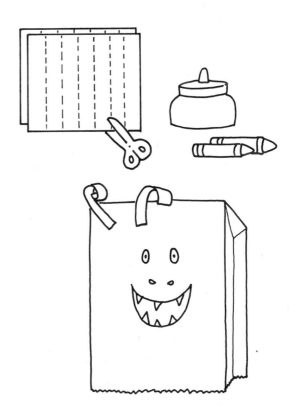

Drawing Lessons For Halloween

A Dancing Witch

This little witch is perfect for hanging in the window to welcome Halloween.

Materials:
white construction paper
black construction paper
orange construction paper
brass paper fasteners
crayons
scissors
glue or paste

Steps to follow:

1. Cut out the head piece first. Cut other pieces to match that size. Cut a round head and hand from the white construction paper.

head   hands

2. Round corners of a black paper square to create a circle. Fold the circle in half and cut on the fold. One half becomes the witch's cape, the other half can be cut to form the hat and boots.

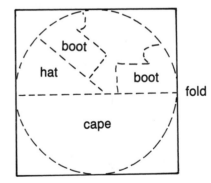

boot

hat   boot   fold

cape

Add hair from orange paper strips. Draw the face with crayons.

3. Cut an orange pumpkin to go in the witch's hand. Paste the hand and pumpkin to the body.
Use paper fasteners to connect the head and boots to the body. Fold the cape around. Hang the witch by a string attached to her hat.

Pumpkins

Magic Vine

A fairy seed I planted,
So dry and white and old
There sprang a vine enchanted
With magic flowers of gold.

I watched it, tended it,
And truly, by and by,
It bore a jack-o'-lantern,
And a great Thanksgiving pie.

Author Unknown

Science Sequencing

Plan a science unit on the growth of a pumpkin. Let
students complete the sequence worksheet on page 86. Be
sure to read *Pumpkin, Pumpkin* by Jeanne Titherington
(Greenwillow Books, 1986).

Pop-Up Life Cycle Book

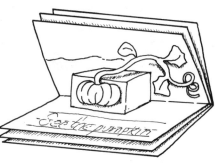

Follow these steps to create a wide pop-up fold.
Each child will need to make four (or six) pop-up pages.
They then draw one step in the life cycle on the pop-up tab
of each page. (Students who are ready can write a
sentence or paragraph about that stage of development.)
Paste the pages together back-to-back and place inside a
construction paper cover.

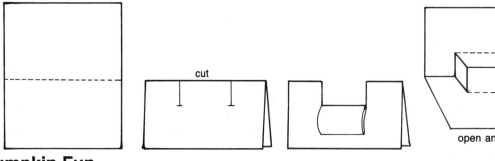

cut

open and reverse fold

Pumpkin Fun

Carve pumpkins into unusual jack-o'-lanterns.
Vary this activity by carving a large zucchini, turnip, or apple
instead of a pumpkin.
Save the seeds! Toast a few to nibble on, but save the rest to
make "Pumpkin Seed Smiles." (See page 85.)
Buy an extra pumpkin to cook. Give your students the chance to
make a pumpkin pie or pumpkin bread from scratch.

How to Plan Your School Year

Pumpkin Seed Smile
Who is it?

Materials:

Large construction paper (any color)

Circle of construction paper in the same color (for the mouth)

Scissors, glue, crayons

Pumpkin seeds

A few quick and easy steps are all that you need to create these spectacular "smiles."

Steps to follow:

1. Fold the circle in half. Glue the pumpkin seeds in a ring around the inside.

2. Close the circle back in half. Paste the half circle in the center of the large construction paper.

3. Now use crayons to finish the fellow's face.
   Who is it anyway?

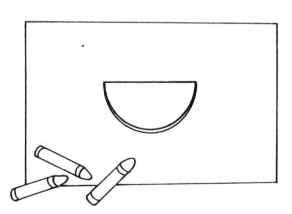

It is fun to write stories about these unusual creatures. Place the stories inside a cover and add it to your library of student produced books. Use one "pumpkin smile" as the front cover.

Pumpkin Life Cycle

1. Color.	2. Cut out.	3. Paste in order.
1	2	3
4	5	6

I can pick the big, orange pumpkin.

See the plant grow.

A little pumpkin starts to grow.

Pumpkin flowers grow on the vine.

Plant the seeds.

Now I have a jack-o'-lantern.

Pumpkin Math

1. Take a pumpkin. Have your students estimate the number of seeds in the pumpkin. Cut open the pumpkin and count the seeds.

   Put the seeds into sets of 5, 10, or 100 for other counting experiences.

   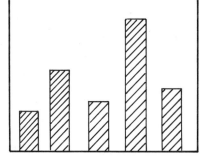

2. Sort pumpkins by size. (Use real pumpkins or cut various sizes from construction paper.)
   a. Put the pumpkins in size order:
      tall to short
      wide to narrow
   b. If you are using real pumpkins:
      weigh them and put in order from heaviest to lightest
      measure the distance around and put them in order of smallest to largest

3. Make bar graphs using questions about pumpkins to gather information.
   a. Does your family carve a jack-o'-lantern for Halloween?
   b. Does your family toast and eat the pumpkin seeds?
   c. Where do you get your pumpkin?
      raised it in our garden
      bought it at a store
      bought it at a pumpkin farm

4. Create word problems about pumpkins.

Tay's pumpkin weighs 5 pounds and Anne's weighs 9 pounds. How much more does Anne's pumpkin weigh than Tay's?

Michael picked out a 7 pound pumpkin. It cost 25 cents a pound. How much did the pumpkin cost?

The pumpkin stand sold 27 pumpkins on Friday, 43 on Saturday, and 36 on Sunday. How many pumpkins were sold in all?

Mrs. Jackson's class had 12 pumpkins. The total weight of the pumpkins was 288 pounds. What was the average weight of each pumpkin?

Bats

Read:

Wild Babies by Irene Brady; Houghton Mifflin, 1979
Bats by Althea; Longman, 1985
The Bat Poet by Randall Jarrell; Macmillan, 1964
A Bat is Born by Randall Jarrell; Doubleday & Co., 1978
Discovering Bats by Jane Mulleneux; Bookwright Press, 1989
Stellaluna by Janell Cannon
Bats by Sylvia A. Johnson
Bats in the Dark by John Kaufmann

A science unit about the unusual habits of bats can be a big success this month. They are a fascinating subject.

ARM

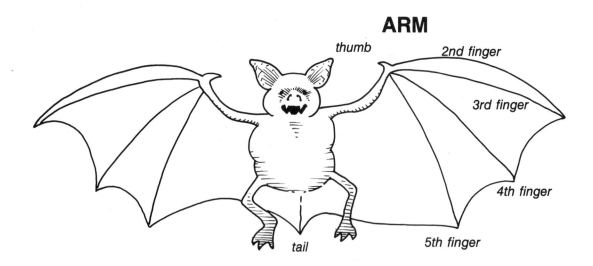

About Bats

Bats are interesting mammals. They can be as small as hummingbirds or have a wingspread of six feet. Some eat fruit or flowers. Others eat frogs, lizards, and fish. Most bats eat insects.

Bats find their way around at night by using a system called *echolocation*. The bat sends out a sound that strikes objects and comes back as an echo. This helps the bat know where the object is located, how far away it is, and if it is moving. Bats that use echolocation have very large ears. However, not all bats use this system. Most fruit bats have small ears and large bulging eyes. These bats usually find their way around by sight. They also use their good sense of smell to help them find food.

What makes bats so special is that they are the only mammal that can truly fly. Bats do not have feathers like birds. They have wings made of thin layers of skin that come out from the sides of the bat's body. This thin membrane is attached to the bones in the bat's arms and hands. In the picture you can see the fingers of the bat's hand. By moving its fingers, the bat can maneuver through the air.

Writing About Bats

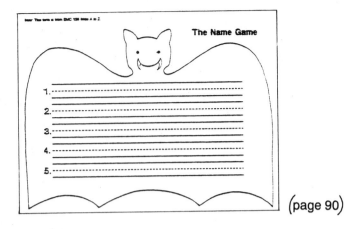

(page 90)

The Name Game

Select a letter.
Each answer must begin with that letter.

1. What is your name?
2. Where do you live?
3. What do you eat?
4. What is your job?
5. What do you like to play?

Example:

Basil Bat
Baltimore
Bloody bugs
Busboy
Baseball

This can be done orally by younger students or in written form by older students. Use the form on page 90 to play the "Name Game."

Awake All Day

Write stories about a little bat that couldn't sleep, so he sets out to explore the daylight world.

Bats in the Attic

Have children try to create a way to go about getting rid of the bats in the attic without hurting them.

       How to Plan Your School Year

The Name Game

1.

2.

3.

4.

5.

Note: This form is from EMC 138 *Write A to Z.*

How to Plan Your School Year

Note: This cover is from EMC 207 *How to Make Books With Children.*

The Big Bat Book

Make a book of alliterative phrases about bats. For example:

busy bats	baby bats	black bats
bashful bats	bushy bats	backward bats

Save the bat stories your students write and bind them into this book.

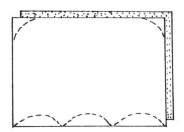

1. Covers

Cut two rectangular sheets of tagboard into the bat shape. (One is black, one is white.)

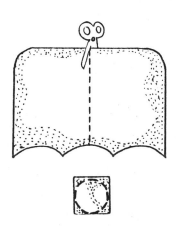

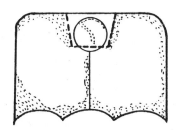

2. Front cover

Cut down the center of the black form.

Cut a circle from black paper for the bat's head. Lay the head on the front cover. Sketch in your cutting lines. Cut on these lines.

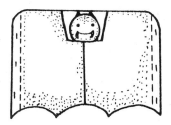

3. Back Cover

Paste the bat's head on the back cover. (This will be the white page.) Cut writing paper to fit below the head. Hold the pages in place with paper fasteners. Add the bat's ears with black felt pen. Glue on little buttons for eyes. Crinkled aluminum foil makes great fangs.

4. Hinge the front cover on the left and the right sides. Staple to the back cover. Cover both edges with cloth tape.

Writing Poetry

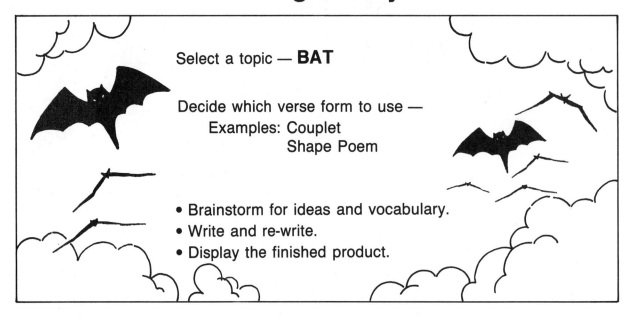

Select a topic — **BAT**

Decide which verse form to use —
  Examples: Couplet
              Shape Poem

- Brainstorm for ideas and vocabulary.
- Write and re-write.
- Display the finished product.

Couplet — a two-line poem that usually rhymes

1. Provide the first sentence about the topic. The complexity of the sentence will depend on the specific needs of your class.

A small black bat

or

Quietly staring, the mysterious bat

2. Brainstorm to create a list of words rhyming with the topic. (This is a great time to use a dictionary or thesaurus if you have students in grades three or higher.)

hat	cat	sat
pat	mat	fat
vat	flat	rat

3. The class creates the second line of the couplet together.

A small black bat
Was chasing a rat.
Quietly staring, the mysterious bat
Flew around where the ghosts and the goblins sat.
Quietly staring, the mysterious bat
Was mesmerized by a passing black cat.

A small black bat
Sat on the witch's hat.

You may choose to have your students copy their favorite couplets and illustrate them to put into a classroom book.

Shape poems — the words follow the basic shape of the poem topic.

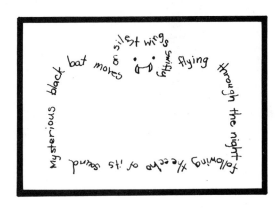

1. Pick an object — **BAT**

2. Draw the outline of the object using black crayon or pen.

3. Describe the object. Make a list of words or phrases about the object. Arrange them in a way that sounds pleasing to you.

> black
> night hunter
> silent wings
> swift flyer
> searching for insects to eat
> following the echoes of his sounds
> mysterious creature

4. Put a plain sheet of paper over the drawing. Clip the papers together with a paper clip so they will not wiggle. Write your description following the shape of the picture.

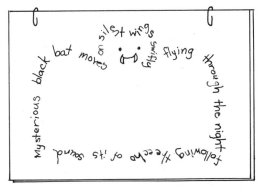

5. Paste the poem to a sheet of colored paper to make a frame.

Activities for November

Other celebrations to plan this month:

November 3 - Sandwich Day
November 6 - John Philip Sousa's Birthday
November 18 - Mickey Mouse's Birthday
Cat Week
National Book Week
Novem"bear" Festival

Authors' November Birthdays:

November 9 - Lois Ehlert	*Color Zoo*
November 14 - William Steig	*Sylvester and the Magic Pebble*
November 25 - Marc Brown	*Pickle Things*
November 27 - Kevin Henkes	*Chrysanthemum*
November 28 - Ed Young	*Lon Po Po: A Chinese Red Riding Hood*

How to Plan Your School Year

Discovering America

Past and Present

Expose your students to discoverers of America, from pre-Columbian explorers to modern immigrants.

Read:
Before Columbus, Who Discovered America? by Harry Edward Neal; Messner, 1981
Who Found America? by Johanna Johnston; Children's Press, 1973
Before Columbus by Muriel Batherman; Houghton Mifflin, 1981

(Here are some sample questions. You will need to select those that are appropriate for your students.)

Who were the first people to explore America? Where did they come from? How did they get to America? Can you think of some reasons why they came?

How did the Vikings find America? Why didn't they stay?

Where was Columbus going when he discovered America? Did he find what he was searching for? What effect did Columbus' discovery have on the settling of the New World?

Why did the Pilgrims come to America? What did they find when they arrived? How was America different from the land they left behind? What was the relationship between the Native Americans and the new settlers?

What effect did the arrival of settlers in America have on the tribes of Native Americans already living in America?

The Pilgrims were not the last people to settle America. Can you name some other groups that came to America as it was being settled? Why do you think these various groups came?

People are still coming to America. Can you name some of the groups of people that are arriving today? Why do you think people are still coming to America?

Where do you think explorers and settlers will go in the generations to come?

Another good source of information is *Cobblestone* magazine. The October, 1984 issue is devoted to articles about the possible discovery of America before Christopher Columbus arrived.

Here are some interesting books about people new to America.
Select several to share with your students.

Molly's Pilgrim by Barbara Cohen; Lothrop, 1983
Hello, My Name is Scrambled Eggs by Jamie Gilson; Simon and Schuster, Inc., 1985
A Boat to Nowhere by Maureen Crane Wartski; The Westminster Press, 1980
How My Parents Learned to Eat by Ina R. Friedman; Houghton Mifflin Co., 1984
To Be a Slave by Julius Lester; Dial, 1968
In the Year of the Boar and Jackie Robinson by Bette Bao Lord; Harper, 1984
How Many Days to America? A Thanksgiving Story by Eve Bunting; Clarion Books, 1988
Making a New Home in America by Maxine Rosenberg; Lothrop, 1986
The Plymouth Thanksgiving by Leonard Weisgard; Doubleday, 1967
The Buck Stops Here by Alice Provensen
...If You Sailed on the Mayflower in 1620 by Ann McGovern
Over the River and Through the Wood: A Song for Thanksgiving by Lydia Maria Child;
Harper Collins, 1993

Time Lines

Make a time line of the discoverers of America. As you discuss a
person or group, make a card listing the date of arrival in
America and the name of the person or group arriving. Pin the
cards in order above your chalkboard.

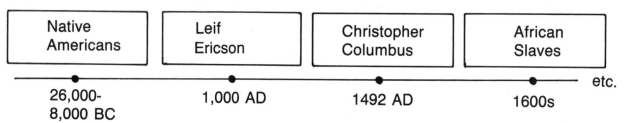

Native Americans	Leif Ericson	Christopher Columbus	African Slaves
26,000-8,000 BC	1,000 AD	1492 AD	1600s

etc.

Make a time line of families in your class. Use the form on page 98.
Have each child take the form home to be filled in with parental help.
When the forms are returned, hang them along a clothesline in order
or pin them up along a bulletin board.

Note: You might tell about your own family to get the class started.

We Came to the U.S.A.

A pilgrim was a traveler to a new land. Many "pilgrims" are still coming. Some came recently; some came long ago, but all our families were once newcomers to the United States of America. Write about your family's journey to this "new" land.

You may have to talk to many people in your family to find the answers to these questions.

When did your family **first** arrive in the U.S.A.?

Where did they come from?

How did they get here?

Who came at that time?

Why did they come?

Where did they settle?

Find the answers to these questions if you can:

What could they bring with them?
How long did the journey last?
What happened on the journey?

Have your parents help you fill in the form on the next page.

       How to Plan Your School Year

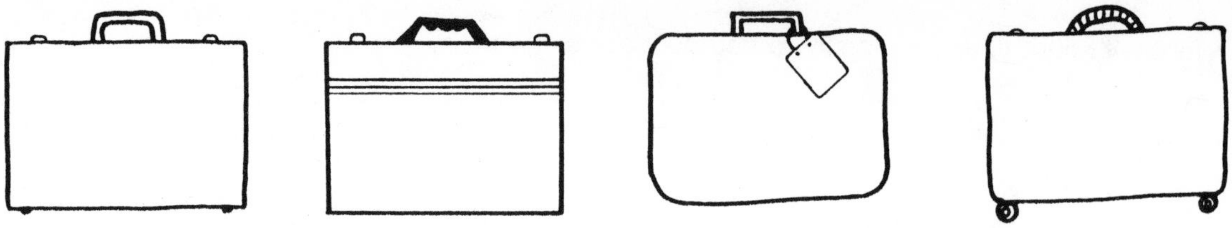

My name is _____

My mother's family name is_____

They came from _____ in _____
                                                              year

Tell about their journey. _____

_____

_____

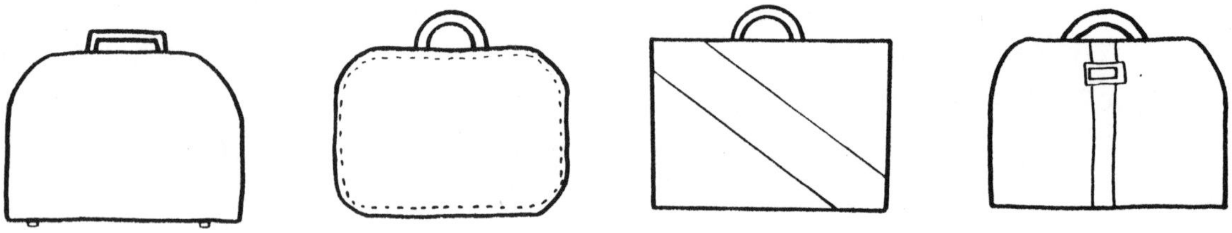

My name is _____

My father's family name is _____

They came from _____ in _____
                                                              year

Tell about their journey. _____

_____

_____

Pilgrims in the 21st Century

The Pilgrims traveled across a vast sea to get to a strange land to start a new life.

Imagine that you are a "pilgrim" traveling through space to start a new life on a strange planet.

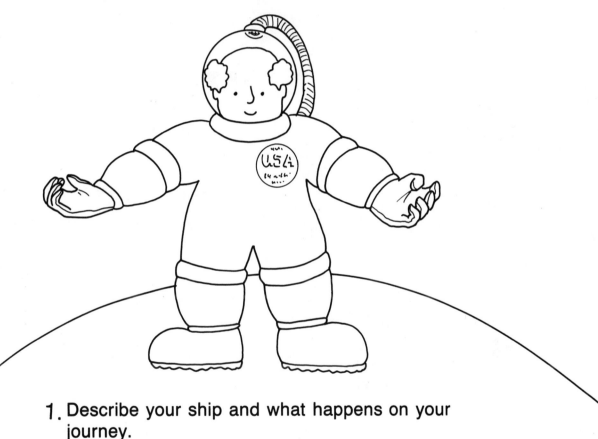

1. Describe your ship and what happens on your journey.

2. Describe the planet and how you would start your new home.

3. Illustrate your new home.

Celebrating Fall Harvests

Since human beings first harvested crops there have been celebrations of thanks. Usually these celebrations included a feast of some sort.

There are many harvest celebrations still occurring throughout the world in various societies. Each celebration has unique features, but the themes of gratitude, recognition of human dependence on nature, and appreciation of the work of those who cultivate the land occur consistently.

In 1621 at Plymouth, the colonists invited Native Americans from the Wapanoag tribe to a feast to celebrate their survival through the winter and to show their gratitude to the Wapanoags for their help in teaching the Pilgrims what to plant, how to grow it, and what to hunt. Squanto (a Patuxet) shared seeds and showed them how to use and prepare food, plants, and meat and how to make shelters. The first feast consisted of venison, leeks, spirits, many varieties of berries, and corn bread.

Writing Activities

- Story Starters

    Describe how your family celebrates a day of thanksgiving.
    Here are five things I am thankful for... (Give a reason for each one.)
    If I could speak to _____, I would ask...
        Squanto   a Pilgrim child   Chief Massasoit
    Pretend you are a Native American trying to explain about popcorn to a Pilgrim who has never seen it before.
    Imagine you are a Native American. How might you feel about Thanksgiving celebrations?

- Titles

    How to Catch a Turkey
    The Smells of Thanksgiving
    Thanksgiving from a Turkey's Point of View
    Squanto, the Pilgrims' Friend
    Gathering Food in 1620

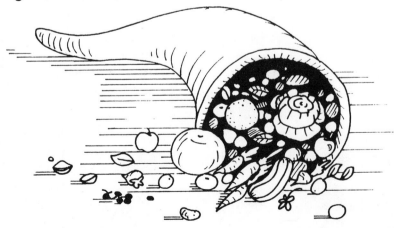

Native American Celebrations

Native Americans had many ceremonies. Some involved only a small group of people (a ceremony for naming a child); others were for an entire village or group of villages (celebrating an abundant harvest). These ceremonies were usually a time of thanksgiving. Many of the celebrations lasted several days. They included many ritual offerings, prayers, and symbolic activities directed by priests or shamans. There were three important parts to these ceremonies — dancing, feasting, and playing games.

> Harvest thanksgiving
> Winter solstice (on or near Dec. 22)
> New Year
> The first day of spring
> Summer solstice (on or near June 22)
> Lunar or solar eclipse
> Native American Day (fourth Friday in September)

If you celebrate any of these actual Native American ceremonies, be respectful of the culture. Don't just imitate dances and activities. They should become an occasion to share and to develop an understanding about Native American cultures.

Plant a Native American Garden

The Iroquois believed that the spirits of three beautiful sisters lived in the fields protecting the crops. One sister looked after corn plants; one sister looked after bean plants; and the third sister looked after squash plants. Corn, beans, and squash were planted close together in one mound. The corn plants growing tall and straight formed a pole for the bean vines to climb and the squash grew around the base of the other two plants. Many Native American tribes grew the same three plants together in this way.

If you have a little space to garden, let your class plant its own "three sisters" plot. Hoe the soil and make small hills two feet apart. Plant a few dried corn kernels, several beans, and some squash seeds in each mound. Add fertilizer if you wish (or add a piece of raw fish in the mound as the Native Americans did). Plant in the spring and harvest in the fall.

(Source unknown)

Native American Foods

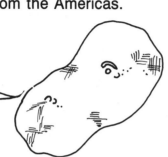

Many of our present foods were unknown to Europeans before Columbus arrived in the New World. Native Americans (especially the Mayas of Central America, the Aztecs of Mexico, and the Incas of Peru) had been growing these plants for hundreds (maybe thousands) of years. Today much of the world's population eats these foods that came originally from the Americas.

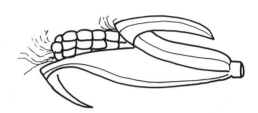

Maize or Corn — The most important food given us by Native Americans was corn. Scientists think there must have been a kind of corn plant growing wild in the areas we call Mexico, New Mexico, and Arizona when the first people reached that part of America thousands of years ago. Explorers were given corn by the Native Americans they met. The first settlers would have starved without the corn and other native foods given them by Native American tribes. After Columbus carried corn seeds back to Spain, it was grown all across Europe. Today corn is used as food for people and animals. Corn by-products are a part of many items we use every day.

Potato — Potatoes came from South America, but they came the long way round to get to North America. The explorer Francisco Pizzaro took potatoes back to Spain. When Spanish colonists settled in Florida they brought potatoes to North America with them. British adventurers took potatoes back home where the British farmers planted them as food for hogs and cattle. The Irish made potatoes a large part of their diet. When the Irish settlers came to America they planted potatoes as food.

Beans — When Columbus discovered the New World, native groups from Chile to Canada were already growing many varieties of beans. European explorers began carrying dry beans aboard ship to supplement the dry corn meal and rotting salt pork that was their usual diet on long journeys. As a result, beans became a popular new food source throughout Europe.

Many other food stuffs originated in parts of the Americas:

    avocado (raised by Incas, Mayans, and Aztecs)

    chocolate and cocoa (West Indies)

    peanuts (Brazil, Uraguay, Paraguay)

    pineapple (Brazil or Central America)

    tomatoes (South and Central America)

    squash and pumpkin (grown throughout the Americas)

    sunflower seeds (grown by Native Americans between the Rocky Mountains and the Atlantic Coast)

Celebrate Winter

Facts about Winter:

• Northern Hemisphere - The approximate months of winter are December, January and February.

• Winter Solstice - December 22 - The sun is as far from Earth as it can get, resulting in the shortest day of the year.

• The South Pole is tilted toward the sun, causing indirect sun rays. These days are shorter and colder.

• During winter, snow collects and can be stored for slow release as water through the rest of the year.

Poems for Winter

Share books and poems about winter with your students.

When winter arrives
 trees change into dark shadows
 in my neighbor's yard.

> J.E. Moore

In freezing weather,
little snowflakes start to fall.
Catch them on your tongue.

> J.E. Moore

In some towns
The birds fly south
And animals sleep in
      burrows below.
In some towns
The leaves all fall
And everything is
      covered with snow.
But...
In my town
The birds still sing
And flowers bloom all year
      in their beds.
In my town
The leaves stay green
And a warm sun shines
      overhead.

> J.E. Moore

Bibliography:

The Mitten by Alvin Tresselt; Lothrop, Lee & Shepard, 1966
Bear Gets Dressed by Harriet Ziefert; Harper & Row, 1986
Weather Forecasting by Gail Gibbons; Macmillan, 1987
Ring of Earth by Jane Yolen; Harcourt Brace Jovanovich, 1986
Stopping By Woods On A Snowy Evening by Robert Frost; Dutton, 1978
Mooncake by Frank Asch; Prentice-Hall, 1983
Winter's Coming by Eve Bunting; Harcourt, 1977
Katy and the Big Snow by Virginia Lee Burton; Houghton, 1943
Plants in Winter by Joanna Cole; Crowell, 1973
A Walk in the Snow by Phyllis Busch; Harper, 1971

Think About It:

Winter is not the same in all parts of the United States. Why? How can weather affect what people can do, how they dress, and the types of homes in which they live? Suppose you were moving from Hawaii to Alaska in the middle of winter. Describe the biggest change in your lifestyle.

Explain which you prefer and why - snowy or sunny weather.
You live where there is no snow. How would you make a "snowman"?
List all of the things you can do during cold winter that you cannot do during warm summer.

Writing Activities:

Write a poem about your favorite part of winter. (Try couplets with young children and haiku with older students.) Write a story about the worst snowstorm in history. Describe the perfect vacation.

   How to Plan Your School Year

Activities for December

Other celebrations to plan this month:

Winter Solstice
December 10 - Hanukkah
December 13 - Santa Lucia
December 16 - Beethoven's Birthday
December 17 thru 25 - Los Posadas/Kwanzaa
December 22 - Happy Birthday Winter

Authors' December Birthdays:

December 1 - Jan Brett	*Annie and the Wild Animals*
December 2 - David Macauley	*Black and White*
December 19 - Eve Bunting	*Scary, Scary Halloween*
December 22 - Jerry Pinkny	*Mirandy and Brother Wind*
December 30 - Mercer Mayer	*There's a Nightmare in My Closet*

Winter Holidays Around the World

Holidays representing many cultures and religions occur during the winter months. You might select several that share a common theme or select those you feel are important for your students to know about. Plan activities that are appropriate to the age and ability of your students. Look for the elements of sharing and caring that occur in these celebrations.

For example:
- Christmas (Christian countries and cultures)
- Winter Solstice (many Native American tribes)
- Kwanzaa (Afro-Americans)
- Hanukkah (Jews)

Think About It

Does everyone in America celebrate Christmas?

Do you or someone you know celebrate a different holiday?

Is one celebration better than another? Why or why not?

Do these different holidays have anything in common?

How do we learn about what holidays mean and how to celebrate them?

Many times gifts are given at celebrations. Why does this happen?

Can you think of a "gift" you can give that would be very special but is not something that can be wrapped in paper and ribbon?

How do you think Santa Claus became a part of Christmas?

How to Plan Your School Year

Christmas

One of the most important days in the Christian year is Christmas, the day set aside to celebrate the birth of Jesus. Share the story of the journey to Bethlehem, his birth in the stable, of the star guiding the Wise Men. Discuss how, while it is a religious holiday for Christians, Christmas has become a time of gift-giving and feasts for many other people also.

Read books about the Christmas season.

Christmas Carol by Sara Teasdale; Holt, 1993

Christmas Gift: An Anthology of Christmas Poems, Songs, and Stories compiled by Charlamae Hill Rollins; Morrow, 1993

Christmas Tree Farm by Sandra Jordan; Orchard, 1993

La Nochebuena South of the Border by James R. Dice; Pelican, 1993 (in Spanish and English)

Holly, Reindeer, and Colored Lights by Edna Barth; Houghton, 1971

The Family Christmas Tree Book by Tomie de Paola; Holiday, 1980

The Fir Tree by Hans Christian Andersen; Harper, 1970

The Cobweb Christmas by Shirley Climo; Harper, 1982

The Clown of God by Tomie de Paola; Harcourt, 1978

Nine Days to Christmas by Marie Ets & Aurora Labastida; Viking, 1959

Mousekin's Christmas Eve by Edna Miller; Prentice, 1965

Pedro, the Angel of Olivera Street by Leo Politi; Scribners, 1946

It's Christmas by Jack Prelutsky; Greenwillow, 1981

The Best Christmas Pageant Ever by Barbara Robinson; Avon, 1972

The Twelve Days of Christmas by Jan Brett; Putnam, 1986

Carl's Christmas by Alexandra Day; Farrar, Straus, Giroux, 1990

Explore how Christmas is celebrated in other countries. For example:

Santa Lucia — Sweden
Early on Santa Lucia's day, the oldest girl in the family, wearing a white robe and a crown of candles, brings coffee and saffron buns to the adults.

Los Posadas — Mexico
For eight nights before Christmas, people re-enact the search of Mary and Joseph for shelter. They go to a home and ask to be let in. The owner of the home refuses at first, then invites them in for a party.

Polish Celebrations
Celebrating begins on Christmas Eve and lasts until January 6th. Straw under the table represents the manger. An empty place is left at the table for any stranger coming to the house. The oldest person at the table takes a bite from a rice wafer symbolizing love of peace. The wafer passes from person to person ending with the youngest child.

Have children who do celebrate Christmas explain what occurs in their families.

Kwanzaa

Kwanzaa is an Afro-American holiday. For seven days activities are organized around seven principles (unity, self-determination, collective work and responsibility, cooperative economics, purpose, creativity, and faith). Each day one of the seven principles is explored and a candle is lit for the principle.

Create murals about Black life in the past and today.
Share poetry and music by Black artists.

Discuss (according to the ability of your students) what each of the principles mean.

Have children design banners in red, black, and green.
red — struggle, black — for Afro-Americans, green — for children (the hope of the future)

Have children in your class who celebrate Kwanzaa explain what their families do.

Let's Celebrate Kwanzaa by Helen Davis Thompson; Gumbs and Thomas Publishers, 1989

The Kwanzaa Coloring Book by Valerie J. R. Banks; Sala Enterprises, 1985 (contains information, maps, activities...not just a coloring book)

Celebrating Kwanzaa by Diane Hoyt-Goldsmith; Holiday, 1993

Hanukkah

Hanukkah is one of many Jewish religious holidays. It honors an ancient struggle against the Syrians who occupied Jerusalem and tried to force the Jews to worship other gods. When the Jews drove the invaders away, they found only enough oil in the temple lamp for one day. Miraculously it lasted for eight days, giving them renewed courage. They celebrate today by lighting candles for eight nights.

Share books about Hannukah with your students.

A Great Miracle Happened There by Karla Kuskin; Harper Collins, 1993
Asher and the Capmakers by Eric A. Kimmel; Holiday, 1993
The Gift by Aliana Brodmann; Simon & Schuster, 1993
Potato Pancakes All Around by Marilyn Hirsh
Hanukkah Money by Sholom Aleichem; Greenwillow, 1978
A Picture Book of Hanukkah by David Adler; Holiday, 1982
The Hanukkah Story by Marilyn Hirsh; Hebrew, 1977
I Love Hanukkah by Marilyn Hirsh; Holiday, 1984
Laughing Latkes by Marilyn Goffstein; Farrar, 1981
Hanukkah, The Festival of Lights by Jenny Koralek; Lothrop, Lee & Shepard, 1987
The Chanukkah Guest by Eric A. Kimmel, Holiday House, 1990

Have a menorah in class and explain how the holiday is celebrated. Make a menorah (using paint, paper, or clay) and write about its significance on Hanukkah.

Teach the children how to play the dreidel game.

Have children who celebrate Hanukkah explain what their families do.

Writing Activities for Winter Holidays

• Interview a friend and write about his/her holiday memory.

_____ at My House
　　　　　　(holiday name)

_____ When I Was a Child
　　　　(holiday name)

• Write about your own memories:

My Earliest _____ Memory
　　　　　　　　　(holiday name)

The Best Part of _____
　　　　　　　　　　　(holiday name)

• Christmas

　Write about the first Christmas:
　　The Wise Men

　　Mary and Joseph

　　The Gifts of the Magi

　Write about Santa Claus:
　　Santa's elves are very upset. A terrible disaster has happened in the toy factory.

　　Christmas Eve is over. Now Santa Claus will...

　　Mrs. Claus has been busy all year. It is her responsibility to...

• Kwanzaa

　The Principle of _____
　(Write about the one you feel is the most important)

　Red, Black, and Green—Symbols of Kwanzaa

　A Family Celebration

　Kwanzaa is almost here and there are no candles to be had. What can we do?

• Hanukkah

　Re-tell the story of the first Hanukkah celebration in the temple after the Syrians had been defeated.

　The Miracle of the Oil

　Grandfather's Menorah

　My First Memory of Hanukkah

　The Best Part of Hanukkah

Gifts for Special Occasions

Think About It

Why do people exchange gifts?

Describe how you feel when you receive a gift.

How do you feel when you give a gift?

Describe the best gift you have ever received.

Can a holiday be fun without a gift exchange?

How many holidays/celebrations can you name where gifts are not given? What makes the holiday or celebration special?

What does "It's the thought that counts" mean?

Brainstorm to create a list of...

ways to give something special to others that are not gifts you have purchased or made.

gifts that children can make instead of buy.

"Gifts of Love" — Help children to realize that actions can be a better gift than things many times. Here is a starter list of ideas. Have your students add to it.

Pull the weeds in the flower beds.

Run an errand.

Deliver a message.

Visit someone who has to stay at home.

Read aloud to someone.

Write a letter.

Invite someone to go some place with you.

Help with a job (sweeping, doing dishes, making the bed).

Take care of a pet for someone on vacation.

Winter Performances

Nothing is more fun for children than to put on a show for their peers or parents. It's not so much fun for the busy teacher. Here are some ideas to make it less painful!

Recitations and choral verse:

Select your favorite poems about winter or a winter holiday. Have your students stand or sit around the stage (or an area in your classroom). Individuals, small groups, or the whole class recite their contribution to the program.

Many plays can be done using the same format. Place main characters up on stools. Arrange remaining students around the stage in small groups. Children them read (or recite) their parts. This eliminates the need for intricate costumes and backgrounds. If you feel the need for something a little more elaborate, add lighting and background music or sound effects.

Short and simple plays:

Select a play suitable for a season, holiday, or unit of study.

• Create an impromptu version of an old familiar fairy tale.

• Find a play with enough parts for your whole class. Try to find one which includes a chorus. More timid students will like the security of someone else helping to say the lines.

• If you cannot find a play that fits your needs, try adapting (another) one. For example, *The Elves and the Shoemaker* can be turned into a play for winter or Christmas by changing a few sentences of dialogue and adding a few appropriate elements to your settings and costumes.

Activities for January

Other celebrations to plan this month:

January 5 - George Washington Carver Day
January 6 - National Nothing Day
January 23 - National Handwriting Day
January 24 - Eskimo Pie patented
January 26 - Carrot Festival
January 27 - Mozart's Birthday
January 31 - Soldag Festival (Norway)

Authors' January Birthdays:

January 4 - Jacob Grimm	*Nursery & Household Tales*
January 5 - Lynn Cherry	*The Great Kapok Tree*
January 7 - Kay Chorao	*Albert's Toothache*
January 10 - Remy Charlip	*Fortunately*
January 12 - Charles Perrault	*Cinderella*
January 18 - A.A. Milne	*Winnie the Pooh*
January 28 - Ann Jonas	*Round Trip*

Special January Celebrations

National Soup Month

Celebrate "Soup" all month long! Use soup labels for alphabetical order and as a border for a "soup-er" bulletin board. Have children graph their favorite kind of soup as well as use their creativity to invent a new one. Bring in cookbooks and have children apply math skills by doubling and halving soup recipes. Make a different kind of soup in a crock pot every Friday.

Soup Books by Robert Newton Peck
Uncle Willy and the Soup Kitchen by DyAnne DiSalvo-Ryan
Stone Soup by (your favorite version)

Hobby Month

Use National Hobby Month as a way to advertise hobbies as well as a way for children to get to know the teachers in your building on a more personal level. Have every teacher make a small display board in the cafeteria or in the hallway outside of his or her room. Coordinate some sharing time and take children through the displays. Use this as a lead-in to creating such a display in the classroom to share students hobbies.

National Carrot Festival

Develop the carrot theme in your classroom. Put up bulletin boards, plant carrot seeds, learn about roots and how they help us, write carrot books. The possibilities go on and on.

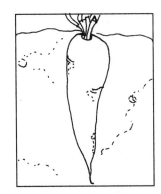

The Carrot Seed by Ruth Krauss
A Silly Tale by Jan Mark

Antarctica/Penguins

January is the perfect time to "visit" Antarctica as part of your geography/ social studies program. Penguins are a natural animal to include at this time.

Antarctica by Helen Cowcher
A Tale of Antarctica by Ulco Glimmerveen
Tacky the Penguin by Helen Lester

       How to Plan Your School Year

A Blizzard of New Year Wishes

How to make:

Background

Back the bulletin board with blue butcher paper.

Snowflakes

1. Fold a square piece of paper.
   (Use lightweight paper.)

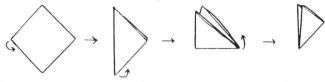

2. Create your own design by cutting away as much as you desire. Open the finished snowflake and check the design. You may need to refold and cut away more paper to achieve a snowflake you like.

3. Scatter the snowflakes across the bulletin board. Pin them in place.

How can this bulletin board change?

A Blizzard of New Year Wishes

Gradually rearrange the snowflakes so that they have all fallen to the bottom of the board creating a snowdrift.

After a day or so, begin to build a snowman. Cut the basic shapes from paper (or use the snowflakes).

Each day add something new to the snowman until he is complete.

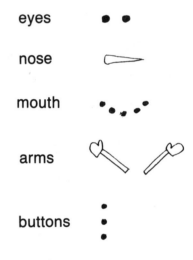

eyes

nose

mouth

arms

buttons

Top him off with a top hat out of someone's closet, or try the lost and found.

A Blizzard of New Year Wishes

Other suggestions:

Post a copy of your favorite snow poem beside the snowman.

Have children write adventures for the snowman. Display these original stories by the snowman.

Have your students write about winter (poem, paragraph, descriptive sentence) on a small circle. Paste the circles into the middle of their snowflakes.

Toboggan Kids

This art lesson can be used on a bulletin board with great success or to add interest to creative stories about winter fun.

Materials:

Reproduce the pattern on the following page on white construction paper.

Brown construction paper (3 1/2'' X 8'') for the toboggan

Crayons

Scissors

Paste

Steps to follow:

1. Color all pattern pieces. Draw the faces. Design sweaters or jackets. Add designs to scarves and caps.

2. Cut out all pieces. Paste a hat and scarf to each person.

3. Curl the end of the toboggan. (A pencil is good for this.)

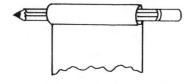

4. Fold the bottom piece of each child under. Fold the arms up. Paste the hands of the front kid to the toboggan. Paste the hands of the back kid to the back of the front kid.

Bulletin board:

Cover the board with blue paper. Attach strips of white butcher paper loosely to the board to form toboggan runs. Tape or glue toboggans to the snow.

Pattern for Toboggan Kids

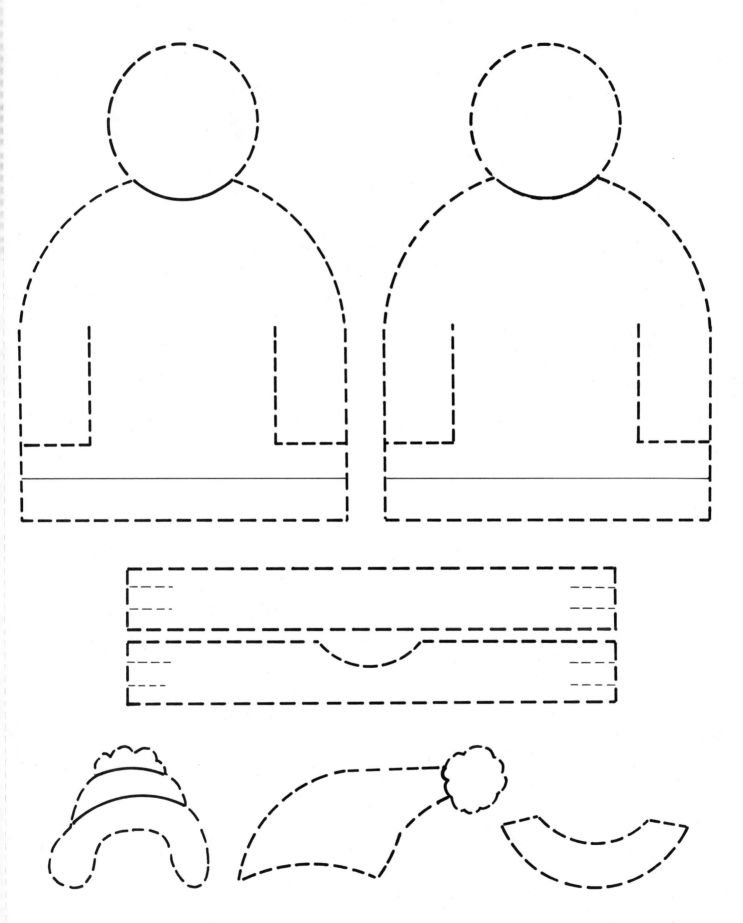

Martin Luther King Day

January 15

Every boy and every girl
    has the right to be free.
Every American can follow a dream,
    from the very old, to children like me.

Free to dream a private dream
    about things we'll grow up to be.
Free to dream a public dream
    about helping preserve democracy.

Martin Luther King dreamed
    that one day his people would be free.
Martin died, but his dream is alive
    in the spirit of children like me.

            Leslie Tryon

I Have a Dream: The Story of Martin Luther King, Jr. by Margaret Davidson; Scholastic Inc., 1986
Martin Luther King Day by Linda Lowery; Carolrhoda Books, 1987
Martin Luther King: Fighter for Freedom by Edward Preston; Doubleday, 1970
Martin Luther King Day by Joyce K. Kessel; Carolrhoda, 1982
A Special Bravery by Johanna Johnston; Dodd, Mea & Company, 1967
Martin Luther King, Jr.: A Picture Story by M. Boone-Jones; Childrens Press, 1968

Think About It :

Why do you think some people want to believe they are better/smarter/stronger than other people just because of skin color, religion, where they are born, or how much money they have?

Martin Luther King, Jr., had a dream of making the world a better place for his people. What do you think would make your world better? How could you help make your dream come true?

How would you describe Martin Luther King, Jr.?
What do you think "non-violent protest" means?

Pretend you are a Black person riding a bus in Montgomery, Alabama **before** the bus boycott. How do you think you would feel? Be the same person **after** the year-long boycott. Describe your feelings now.

How do you think Dr. King's wife and children felt during the time of the boycotts and marches?

Writing Activities:

- Story Starters
  Use one of the "Think About It"
  questions as motivation
  for writing a story.

- Titles
  A Man With a Dream
  The March on Washington
  Martin Luther King, Jr.'s Family

Read Martin Luther King, Jr.'s "I have a dream" speech to older students.

 How to Plan Your School Year

How to Plan Your School Year

Activities for February

Other celebrations to plan this month:

February 1 - No Talk Day
February 4 - Halfway Winter "White" Picnic
February 15 - Galileo's Birthday
Black History Month
American Chocolate Week
National Friendship Week

Authors' February Birthdays:

February 1 - Jerry Spinelli	*Maniac Magee*
February 2 - Judith Viorst	*I'll Fix Anthony*
February 10 - Stephen Gammell	*Song and Dance Man*
February 11 - Jane Yolen	*Owl Moon*
February 15 - Norman Birdwell	*Clifford, the Big Red Dog*
February 17 - Robert Newton Peck	*Soup*

Special February Celebrations

Dental Health Month

Begin the month with a discussion of Dental Health. Have a local dentist come to your classroom and talk to the children about proper care of their teeth. Have your children make "brushing charts" in the shape of large toothbrushes to take home and put in their bathrooms to remind them to brush.

Pie Month

Now that teeth are in good shape, move on to National Pie Month. This is a fun one-day activity. Have children graph their favorite pie and invent a new one complete with a recipe. Use the poem "Alligator Pie" to create your own version in pop-up form.

Black History Month

Use this as a motivation to move geographically into Africa. Share stories of Anansi the spider. Check out books on Black leaders from your school library to share during the month. Invite people from your community to share about their lives as Black Americans.

> *Let Freedom Ring: A Ballad of Martin Luther King, Jr.* by Myra Cohn Livingston; Holiday, 1992
> *Mary McLeod Bethune* by Eloise Greenfield, Harper Collins; 1977
> *Jackie Robinson: He Was the First* by David A. Adler; Holiday, 1989
> *All Us Come Cross the Water* by Lucille Clifton; Holt, 1973
> *Now Let Me Fly: The Story of a Slave Family* by Delores Johnson; Macmillan, 1993
> *Harriet and the Promised Land* by Jacob Lawrence; Simon & Schuster, 1993

Chocolate Lovers Day

Eat chocolate. Learn about where chocolate comes from. Make "chocolate" finger paintings with chocolate pudding.

> *From Cocoa Bean to Chocolate* by Ali Mitgutsch
> *A Big Fat Pie* by Pat Edwards

Groundhog Day

Read about groundhogs...

The New House by Lorinda Bryan Cauley; Harcourt, 1981
Wake Up, Groundhog! by Carol Cohen; Crown, 1975
This is the Day by John Hamberger; Holiday, 1971
Will Spring Be Early? by Crockett Johnson; Crowell, 1959
Nothing Sticks Like a Shadow by Ann Tompert; Houghton, 1984
It's Groundhog Day! by Steven Kroll; Holiday, 1987

Max is a groundhog
Who has the say-so,
As to the time
That winter will go.

He spends all winter long
In the ground fast asleep.
Then on February second
He comes up for a peek.

He comes out of his hole
And looks all around
To see if his shadow
Appears on the ground.

If he sees his shadow,
Winter will stay.
If there isn't a shadow,
Spring's on the way.

Leslie Tryon

Think About It:

"Can an animal really know what the weather is
going to be?"

"How do you think the idea of groundhogs forecasting
weather started?"

"Groundhogs live underground. Can you name any other
animals that live underground? What kind of homes do they
make? Why might an animal have an underground home?"

"What do these words mean — shadow, burrow, hibernate,
prediction?"

How to Plan Your School Year

Writing Activities

• Story Starters

Lynn the groundhog was afraid of shadows. February the second was almost here! What could she do?

Sarah was a brave little groundhog. She...

We waited and waited, but the groundhog didn't come out. What could have happened?

Pretend you are a groundhog about to peek out of your burrow on Groundhog Day. What happens?

• Story Titles

The Timid Groundhog

A Pest in My Garden

Shadows

Shadow Patrol

Keep your own weather watch. Go outside on February second and observe conditions. Do you see your shadow? Why? Does this have any meaning as far as future weather is concerned?

Groundhog Puppet

February 2 is Groundhog Day.

What fun to watch Groundhog peek out of his hole. Use the puppet to reinforce all the information you teach about the significance of Groundhog Day.

Materials:

- Reproduce the patterns on this and the following page.
- Tongue depressor
- Crayons, scissors, paste
- Stapler

Steps to follow:

1. Cut the dotted lines to create grass. Cut the slit on the fold line. Fold up on the line. Staple the sides. Now color the sun yellow and the grass green.

2. Cut out the cloud. Decide if it will cover part of the sun or not. Paste it in place.

3. Color, then cut out the groundhog. Paste him to a tongue depressor. Slip the other end of the tongue depressor through the slit. Make sure the groundhog pops up and down.

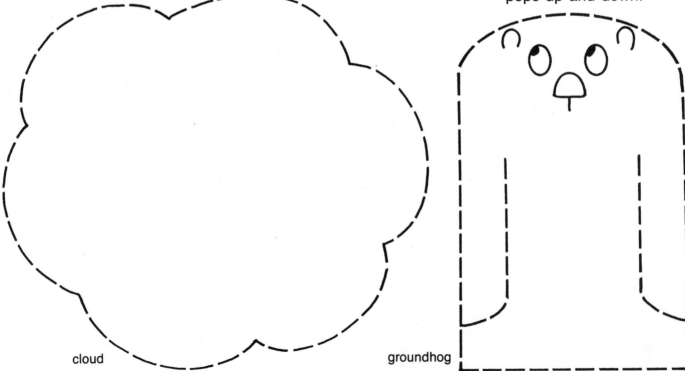

cloud

groundhog

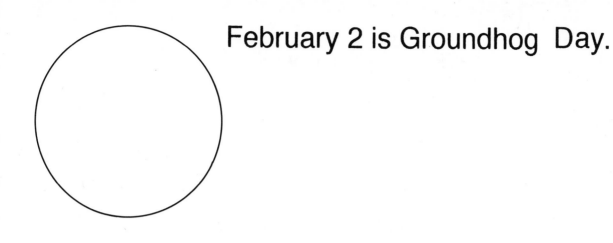

February 2 is Groundhog Day.

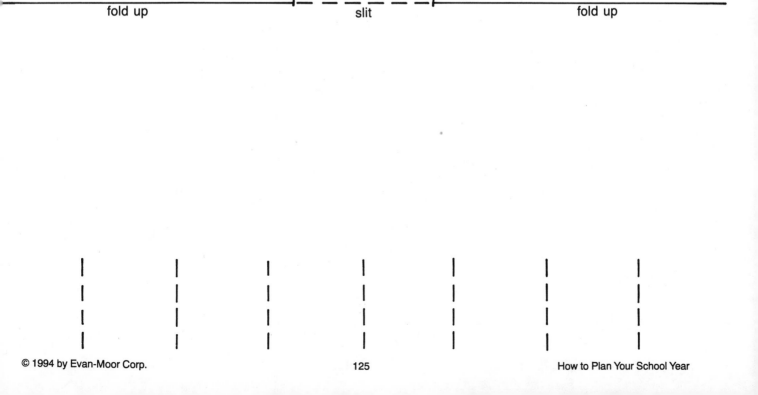

fold up   slit   fold up

How to Plan Your School Year

Chinese New Year
"Gung Hay Fat Choy"

The date varies, but this celebration of the end of winter usually occurs in February. It lasts many days with feasts, parades and gift giving.

The Chinese New Year by Cheng Hou-tien; Holt, Rinehart and Winston.
Chinese New Year by Tricia Brown and Fran Ortiz
Lion Dancer: Ernie Wan's Chinese New Year by Kate Waters and M. Slovenz
Why Rat Comes First by Clara Yen and Hideo Yoshida
Gung Hay Fat Choy by June Brothers

Dragon Headband:

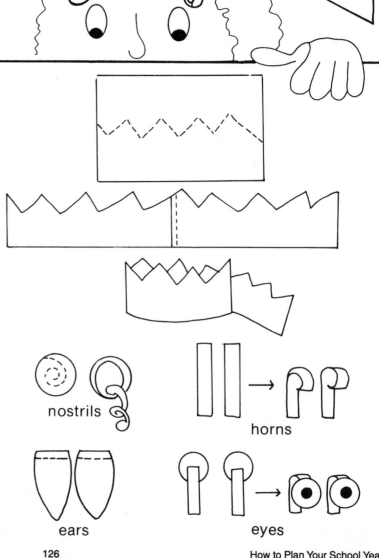

Steps to follow: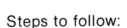

1. Cut a 12" x 18" sheet of green construction paper in zigzag cuts down the center of the paper.
2. Glue these pieces together to form the dragon.
3. Staple the headband to fit each student. Let the left-over hang down to become the dragon's tail.
4. Cut the rest of the dragon from colorful scraps of construction paper. Yellow, magenta and orange are good choices.

   Glue these pieces to the dragon.

   Enjoy your parade!

nostrils

horns

ears

eyes

Valentine's Day

Share these books about Valentine's Day with your students.

Things to Make and Do for Valentine's Day by Tomie de Paola; Watts, 1976
Hearts, Cupids and Red Roses: The Story of the Valentine Symbols by Edna Barth; Houghton, 1982
Good Morning to You, Valentine by Lee Bennett Hopkins; Harcourt, 1976
It's Valentine's Day by Jack Prelutsky; Greenwillow, 1983
The Valentine Bears by Eve Bunting: Houghton, 1983
A Sweetheart for Valentine by Lorna Balian; Abingdon, 1979
Arthur's Valentine by Marc Brown; Little, 1983
The Best Valentine in the World by Marjorie Weinman Sharmat; Holiday, 1982
My First Valentine's Day Book by Marian Bennett & Pan Peltier; Childrens Press, 1985
But Will You Be My Valentine? by Nancy Barth & Sally Wittenborn; Country Schools Publications, 1987
Freckles & Willie: A Valentine's Day Story by Margery Cuyler; Henry Holt and Co., 1986

Good morning to you, Valentine;
Curl your locks as I do mine,
One before and two behind
Good morning to you, Valentine.

Traditional English Rhyme

February 14 is the day
Pretty cards are sent to say
Will you be mine
Pretty Valentine?

J.E. Moore

Activities for Valentine's Day

• Write Your Own Valentine Rhymes

Guide your students through the steps to write simple
verses. Put these verses into greeting cards for sharing with
special friends or family members on Valentine's Day.

• Create funny "love bugs" or charming heart baskets for a
different type of valentine.

Write Your Own Valentine Rhymes

Couplet: 2 lines that rhyme

Will you be mine
Funny Valentine?

Triplet: 3 lines that rhyme

This little heart is a sign
That come rain or sunshine
I want you for my Valentine

Quatrain: 4 lines that can rhyme in several ways:

| 1, 2 | 1, 3 | 1, 4 |
| 3, 4 | 2, 4 | 2, 3 |

February 14 is the day
Pretty cards are sent to say
Will you be mine
Pretty Valentine?

I like Paul
and I like Lou
But...most of all
I like YOU!

I made this Valentine
Flowers and lace
Hearts in place.
It asks if you'll be mine.

Create your own rhyme.

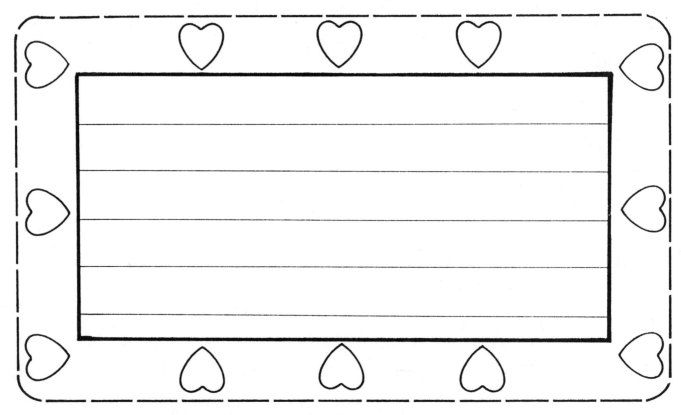

Give it to a special friend.

How to Plan Your School Year

Heart Baskets

These delightful baskets are easy to create from construction paper. They will hold a small valentine treat for a special friend.

Each student will need two 4'' squares, one red or pink and one white. They each will also need a 1'' X 9'' strip of red or pink for a handle.

Steps to follow:

1. Round off the corners of each square to form circles.

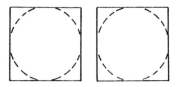

2. Fold each circle in half.

3. Put the two circles together as illustrated and paste the outside pieces together.

4. Paste the handle on the basket.

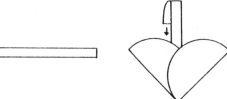

Note: You can use the same pattern to create Christmas ornaments. Make the circles from green and red squares.

How to Plan Your School Year

George Washington and Abraham Lincoln

Read books about the presidents.

George Washington and the Birth of Our Nation by Milton
Meltzer; Watts, 1986

Lincoln: A Photobiography by Russell Freedman; Clarion, 1987

If You Grew Up with George Washington by Ruth Belov Gross;
Scholastic, 1982

If You Grew Up with Abraham Lincoln by Ann McGovern;
Scholastic, 1985

George Washington's Breakfast by Jean Fritz; Coward, 1969

The Abraham Lincoln Joke Book by Beatrice Schenk Regniers;
Scholastic, 1965

True Stories About Abraham Lincoln by Ruth Belov Gross;
Scholastic, 1965

Think About It

How were the lives of Lincoln and Washington different?
What words would you use to describe Washington's
(Lincoln's) character?
Compare and contrast daily life in Washington's (Lincoln's)
time with your life today.

Writing Activities

- Describe Abraham Lincoln (or George Washington).
- Write about Lincoln's (or Washington's)...

        childhood   years as president
        education   family members

- Explain why you do or do not think Lincoln (Washington)
  was a great president.

Draw the Presidents

George Washington and Abraham Lincoln

Write these facts next to the correct picture:

1st president of the USA
16th president of the USA
called "Honest Abe"
called "Father of his Country"
was a farmer and surveyor
was a rail-splitter and lawyer
born in Virginia on Feb. 22, 1732
born in Kentucky on Feb. 12, 1809

his family plantation was called Mt. Vernon
he grew up in a log cabin
married Martha Dandridge
married Mary Todd
General in the Revolutionary War
President during the Civil War
shot and killed in 1865
died of illness in 1799

Celebrate Spring

Facts about Spring:

• Northern Hemisphere - The approximate months of spring are March, April and May.

• Spring Equinox - March 21
The sun is directly over the equator. This causes days and nights of equal lengths.

• During spring, the changes in length of light and dark causes animals to produce eggs. This is good timing, as the young will grow during a period of warmth, abundant food and flowing water.

• Migrating animals head north.

• Spring causes snow to melt causing seeds to begin to sprout.

Poems for Spring

March winds

And April showers

Bring forth

May flowers.

Unknown

I often sit and wish
        that I
Could be a kite up in
        the sky,
And ride upon the breeze
        and go
Whichever way I chanced
        to go.

Anonymous

The March Winds

I come to work as well as play,
        I'll tell you what I do;
I whistle all the live-long day,
        Woo-oo-oo! Woo-oo!

I toss the branches up and down
        And shake them to and fro,
I whirl the leaves in flocks of
        brown
And send them high and low.

I strew the twigs upon the
        ground,
The frozen earth I sweep;
I blow the children round and
        round
And wake the flowers from
        sleep.

Anonymous

135   How to Plan Your School Year

Activities for March

Other celebrations to plan this month:

1st week - Pig Week
March 3 - 10 - Muffin Week
March 7 - Arbor Day
March 24 - Iditarod Race
Hina Matsuri - Japanese Doll Festival

Authors' March Birthdays:

March 2 - Dr. Seuss   *Horton Hears a Who*
March 3 - Patricia MacLachlan   *Sarah, Plain and Tall*
March 6 - Mem Fox   *Possum Magic*
March 11 - Ezra Jack Keats   *The Snowy Day*
March 20 - Mitsumasa Ano   *Topsie Turvies*
March 20 - Lois Lowry   *Number the Stars*
March 20 - Louis Sachar   *There's a Boy in the Girls' Bathroom*
March 28 - Byrd Baylor   *I'm in Charge of Celebrations*

How to Plan Your School Year

Special March Celebrations

National Poetry Month

Even though you have been using poetry all year, March is a great month to emphasize it in honor of National Poetry Month. Use poetry for handwriting and book making. Have your students collect their favorite poems for their own personal poetry anthology. Read poetry, write poetry, illustrate poems, etc. Have a truly "poetic" month.

National Pig Week

There are "tons" of pig books to choose from, so go "Hog Wild"! Read as many different versions of *The Three Little Pigs* as you can find. Compare and contrast. Act it out. Create your own version, maybe even a rap. Share Jon Sciezia's version written from the wolf's point of view, then have children rewrite another fairy tale from a different point of view. Make piggy banks out of large bleach bottles, then practice money skills and concepts.

Pigericks by Arnold Lobel
Pig a Plenty, Pigs Galore by David McPhail
Tommy at the Grocery Store by Bill Grossman
The Piggy in the Puddle by Charlotte Pomerantz
Piggybook by Anthony Browne
The Story of Money by Betsy Maestro
The Go-Around Dollar by Barbara Johnston Adams

National Potato Week

Potatoes and St. Patrick's Day are a splendid combination. Use potatoes for map skills, tracking the potato from its origin in the New World as it moves from one continent to another. Don't forget to make potato prints, eat potatoes, and grow potatoes in a barrel.

In Like a Lion

flip

March comes in like a lion and out like a lamb. (Or vice-versa!) Your class will never forget that old saying after they make this "flip-around" puppet.

Materials:
- Paper plates -
    Two 6 1/2" (15 cm) plates per puppet
- Tongue depressor
- 1 1/2" (4 cm) orange tissue squares - 20 per lion
- Cotton balls
- Construction paper
    black 1 1/2 " x 2 1/2" (4 x 6 cm) - lamb ears
    yellow 1/2" X 1/2" (2 x 2 cm) - lion ears
    red 1" x 1" (2.5 x 2.5 cm) - lamb nose
- Crayons or tempera paint
- Glue

Steps to follow:

1. Lion (use the underside of the plate)
    a. Color the surface with the side of a yellow crayon or paint with yellow tempera paint.

    b. Sketch the face lightly with a pencil. Then trace with a darker color crayon.
    c. Cut the ears from yellow paper. Glue to the plate.

    d. Wrap orange tissue paper squares over a pencil eraser, dip them in glue and set around the edge of the lion's face.

2. Lamb (use the underside of the plate).
    a. Color the lamb's face gray with crayon or paint with tempera paint.

b. Cut ears from black paper and glue to the plate.

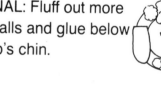

c. Cut the red nose out and glue in place.
d. Color the eyes black.

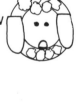

e. Glue a nest of cotton balls above the ears.
    OPTIONAL: Fluff out more cotton balls and glue below the lamb's chin.

3. Turn the lion and lamb upside down on the table. Place a ring of glue around the top edge of both plates.

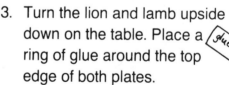

Lay the tongue depressor on one side at the lower mid-point of the puppet. Place the other plate on top and press down until the glue sets.

The Windy Month

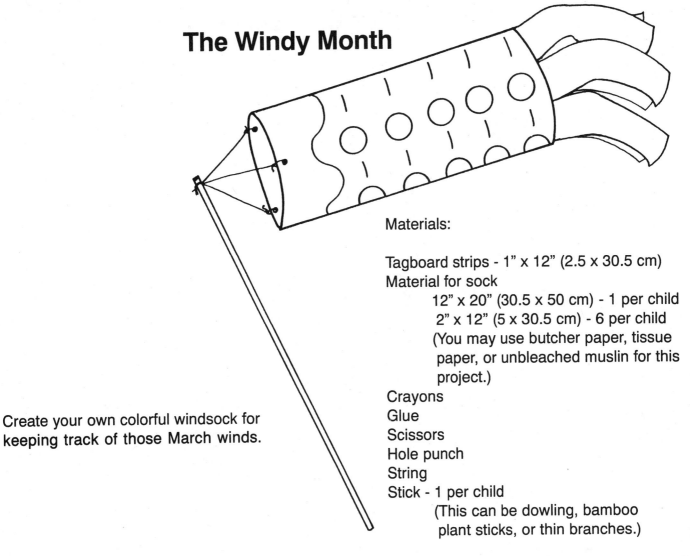

Create your own colorful windsock for keeping track of those March winds.

Materials:

Tagboard strips - 1" x 12" (2.5 x 30.5 cm)
Material for sock
    12" x 20" (30.5 x 50 cm) - 1 per child
    2" x 12" (5 x 30.5 cm) - 6 per child
    (You may use butcher paper, tissue
    paper, or unbleached muslin for this
    project.)
Crayons
Glue
Scissors
Hole punch
String
Stick - 1 per child
    (This can be dowling, bamboo
    plant sticks, or thin branches.)

Steps to follow:

1. Form a ring by stapling the tag strip.

2. Decorate your material with crayons. If paper, just draw your designs. If cloth, draw your design with wax crayon, cover with newspaper and press with a warm iron to set the color. (Teacher needs to do this for younger students.)

3. Glue the windsock together to form a tube. Glue strips to the end. Glue the ring inside the front to keep it open.

4. Make three holes in the ring end with a hole punch. Tie 15" (40 cm) strings to each hole. Tie the other end to your stick.

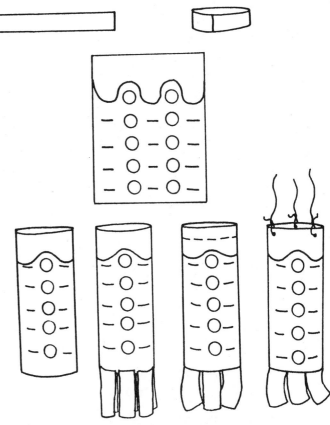

How to Plan Your School Year

St. Patrick's Day

Read:

Leprechauns Never Lie by Lorna Balian; Abingdon, 1980
Shamrocks, Harps and Shillelaghs by Edna Barth; Seabury
Press, 1977
The Hungry Leprechaun by Mary Calhoun; William
Morrow & Co., 1962
St. Patrick's Day in the Morning by Eve Bunting; Clarion
Books, 1980

Activities

1. Locate Ireland on a map.
2. See what information your students can find on Ireland and its people in the school library.
3. Determine the number of children in your class of Irish background. Graph the results.
4. Eat "green" things (sprouts on buttered crackers, pistachio pudding, raw green veggies and green dip).
5. Learn an Irish song and dance an Irish jig.

Shamrock Potato Prints

This shamrock bag has a long list of uses:

1. A trap for leprechauns.

2. A bag to carry the leprechaun's gold home.

3. A special lunch bag for Saint Patrick's Day. (Take along a snack for the leprechaun!)

Materials:
Brown grocery bags
Potatoes
Knives
Tempera paint — green
                  white
Pencils with erasers
Shamrock cookie cutter
Saucers
Paper towels

Steps to follow:

1. Slice a potato in half. Press the cookie cutter into the cut end. Trim off the extra potato with a knife.

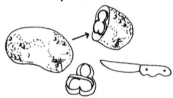

2. Put puddles of paint in saucers. Dip the shamrock potato into the green paint, dab excess off on the paper towel. Press the potato onto the bag.

3. Use a pencil eraser dipped in white paint to add dots.

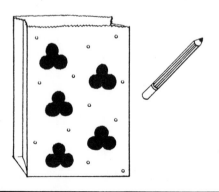

Cross-legged Leprechaun

Fill this delightful leprechaun's pocket with shamrocks containing spelling words, math practice cards, story starters, or candy "gold coins" for a treat on Saint Patrick's Day.

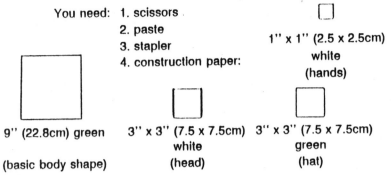

You need:
1. scissors
2. paste
3. stapler
4. construction paper:

1" x 1" (2.5 x 2.5cm) white (hands)

9" (22.8cm) green (basic body shape)

3" x 3" (7.5 x 7.5cm) white (head)

3" x 3" (7.5 x 7.5cm) green (hat)

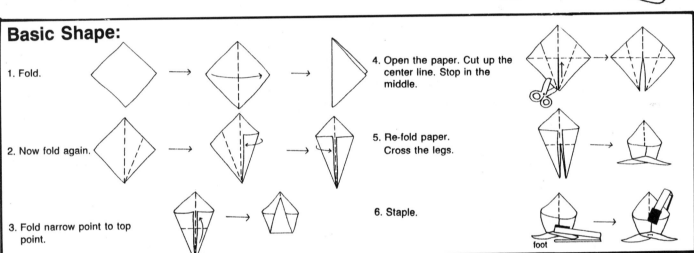

Basic Shape:

1. Fold.

2. Now fold again.

3. Fold narrow point to top point.

4. Open the paper. Cut up the center line. Stop in the middle.

5. Re-fold paper. Cross the legs.

6. Staple.

foot

Head

1. Round the corners on the big white square to make the head.

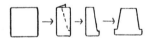

2. Fold the small green paper in the middle. Hold the fold and draw this line.
   Paste the hat on Leprechaun's head.

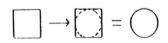

3. Draw the hair and face with your crayons.

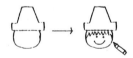

4. Paste the face to the basic body shape.

Body Parts

1. Round the corners on the small white square.
   Paste the hands on the basic shape.
   Use your crayons to draw the sleeves.

2. Curl Leprechaun's toes on a pencil.

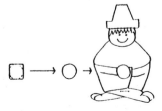

Note: Many variations of this activity can be found in EMC 111 *Cross-legged Critters.*

© 1994 by Evan-Moor Corp.

141

How to Plan Your School Year

Draw Leprechauns

Follow these steps to draw leprechauns in action. Create a background for your picture that tells a story.

Here are the basic poses:

Arms raised in song

Turning a cartwheel

Cross-legged

Dancing a jig

Now add details:

Face

Clothing

How to Plan Your School Year

Note: This project is from EMC 207 *Making Books With Children*.

Peek Under the Mushroom

A Book to Make With Children

1. Begin with yellow construction paper for the background.

2. Cut a mushroom shape from white construction paper. Fold back the top of the mushroom.

3. Paste this flap to the right side of the yellow paper.

   Save the left side of the paper for the story about the mushroom. Paste (or staple) it on when it's completed.

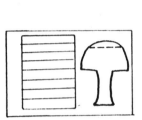

4. Add details to the picture that add interest and enrich the story. Lift the mushroom flap and draw a surprise under it.

5. Collect pages from several students. Add a cover and staple it together on the left. Cover the spine with cloth tape.

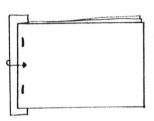

Story Starters:

All his life Timothy had heard that leprechauns hide their fortunes. He was determined to locate some of that treasure. All he had to do was capture one of the tiny green fellows.

I never realized how exciting my family's vacation in Ireland was going to be, until...

I found a fairy circle of mushrooms in the moonlight. When I peeked under the biggest one I found...

The hungry leprechaun wanted some good Irish stew. He took out his favorite pot, filled it with water and started adding...

One spring evening, Tova spied a wee leprechaun racing across her backyard. She...

     How to Plan Your School Year

First Day of Spring

You can't help but feel the excitement of this season. Everything is new and blooming! Plan units on plants or baby animals, plan a unit on the weather to develop the old saying...April showers bring May flowers. Emphasize math skills by skip counting seeds as you plant them or practice adding the blossoms that appear on different plants. Look around your room and see what resources you have overlooked....do you have room for a paint center so that students can paint the beauty they are seeing in nature?

Spring Story by Jill Barklem; Putnam's, 1980
The Boy Who Didn't Believe in Spring by Lucille Clifton; Dutton, 1970
Will Spring Be Early? by Crockett Johanson; Crowell, 1959
The Happy Day by Ruth Krauss; Harper, 1949
The Touch that Said Hello by Victoria Forrester; Atheneum, 1982
Spring by Richard Allington & Kathleen Krull; Raintree, 1981
Why Do Seasons Change? by Dr. Philip Whitfield & Joyce Pope; Viking, 1987
The Winter Wren by Brock Cole; Farrar, Straus & Giroux; 1984
Eat the Fruit, Plant the Seed by Millicent E. Selsam; Morrow, 1980

Think About It

List all of the changes that occur in springtime.
Compare how you feel in springtime with how you feel during winter.
Which season of the year is your favorite? Why?
What does "spring fever" mean?

Writing Activities

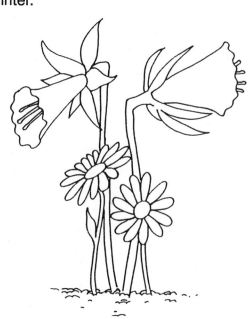

• Story Starters
  The best/worst thing about spring is...
  Write a story that describes a spring rain.
  Pretend you are a baby bird about to take your first flight.

• Titles
  How Spring Got Its Name
  Carried Away by the Wind
  My Life and Times by Rudy Raindrop

 How to Plan Your School Year

Spring Banner

Hang lovely banners to bring a bit of spring into your classroom.

Materials:
Colored butcher paper — 12'' X 24''
(or non-glossy shelf paper)
Watercolors and brushes
Black felt pen — fine point
Yarn — 30'' pieces

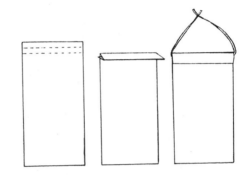

Steps to follow:

1. Fold the top and bottom of your paper under twice (about 1'' each time).
2. Place yarn under the top fold. Glue the fold down. Tie the yarn ends together.
3. Paint a spray of spring flowers down your banner, leaving room to write your spring verse.
4. Write a spring verse or copy a short spring poem you like. Use your best handwriting. Copy the poem with a black felt pen.

Write seasonal poems with your students. Guide them through the steps together. When they feel comfortable with the form you are using, turn them loose to create on their own. For example:

Triplet

Watch my rainbow kite
Sailing high in flight.
What a pretty sight!

Troy

Quatrain

The fog is gray
As smoke rising high.
The fog is quiet
As a cat passing by.

Juan

Haiku

Tiny hummingbirds
dart from flower to flower.
Rainbows in motion.

Stella

Activities for April

Other celebrations to plan this month:

April 1 - April Fools' Day
April 2 - International Children's Book Day
April 23 - Book and Lover's Day
Saint George's Day in Spain
Safety Pin patented (Walter Hunt, 1849)
National Humor Month

Authors' April Birthdays:

April 2 - Amy Schwartz   *The Purple Coat*
April 6 - Graeme Base   *Animalia*
April 12 - Beverly Cleary   *Ramona*

Special April Celebrations

Earth Day - April 22

Make April Earth Month in your classroom. Discuss pollution, ecology and endangered species.

There are many wonderful books to use throughout this theme of study. *The Wartville Wizard* is a great one to get you started. After reading and discussing the book, give every child a lunch bag to decorate as a litter bag. Take a walk around your playground or neighborhood picking up trash. Make a giant person out of butcher paper. Have children glue their collected litter on this "person" and display it in the hallway to demonstrate how much litter was found in the immediate area.

> *The Wartville Wizard* by Don Madden
> *Just a Dream* by Chris Van Allsburg
> *Hey! Get Off Our Train* by John Burningham
> *Agatha's Feather Bed* by Carmen Agra Deedy
> *Old Turtle* by Douglas Wood
> *A River Ran Wild* by Lynn Cherry
> *The Man Who Planted Trees* by Jean Giono

Book and Lover's Day

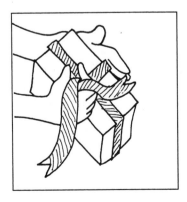

This celebration occurs every year on April 23rd in Spain. Have your children create their own books. (You'll need to start well in advance of April 23rd!) Have each child make a flower and on that special day present the book and the flower to someone they "love." The book and flower could be for family members, classroom friends or your big/little buddies.

Cambodian New Year - April 14

Discuss the customs in other parts of the world. Let children discover the similarities that exist between cultures in their holiday traditions.

> *New Year* by Sothea Chiemruom

April Showers
A Unit About Weather

Read:

Weather and Its Work by David Lambert & Ralph Hardy; Facts on File, Inc., 1984

Weather Forecasting by Gail Gibbons; Macmillan, 1987

The Usborne Book of Weather Facts by Anita Ganeri; EDC Publishing, 1987

A walk in the rain by Ursel Scheffler; G.P. Putnam's Sons, 1984

More Science Secrets by Judith Conaway; Troll, 1987

Rain by Peter Spier; Doubleday & Co., 1982

Let's Try it Out...Wet and Dry by Seymour Simon; McGraw-Hill, 1969

Bear Gets Dressed by Harriet Ziefert; Harper & Row, 1986

Cloudy with a Chance of Meatballs by Judi Barrett; Atheneum, 1980

Feel the Wind by Arthur Dorros; Thomas Y. Crowell, 1989

That Sky, That Rain by Carolyn Otto; Thomas Y.Crowell, 1990

Weather Watch by Valerie Wyatt; Addison Wesley, 1990

What Will the Weather Be Like Today? by Paul Rogers; Greenwillow, 1989

1. Use pictures of weather or seasonal activities as a starting point for descriptive paragraphs. Encourage children to try to make their descriptions so clear that anyone reading them can "feel" the experience with all of their senses.

2. Explain what you think this means...
   "If March comes in like a lion, it will go out like a lamb."
   "March winds and April showers bring forth May flowers."
   "It's raining cats and dogs."

Discuss

Name some of the different types of weather.

Describe the type of clothing you should wear _____.

      on a rainy day   when it snows

      when it is very hot   when a cold wind is blowing

What are some ways we can find out what the weather will be like?

Compare and contrast weather in different habitats around the world.

What are some of the ways animals deal with weather changes?

Describe how weather affects_____.

      occupations   our homes

      recreational activities   our clothing

      transportation   our food sources

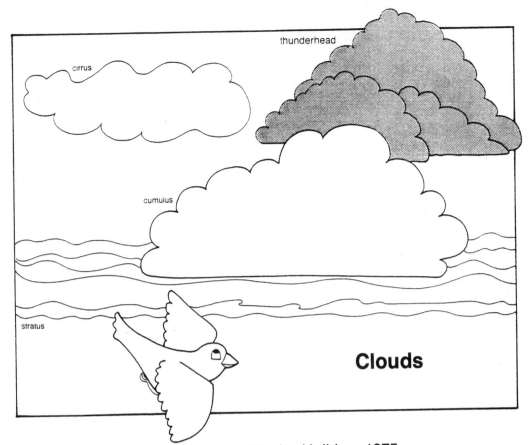

Clouds

The Cloud Book by Tomie de Paola; Holiday, 1975

When warm, damp air meets cold air, the water vapor turns into little drops of water. When millions of the little drops come together they make a cloud.

Clouds can have different numbers of water drops in them. White, thin clouds have a little water. Dark, heavy clouds have a lot of water. Fog is a thin cloud of little drops that come to the ground.

Water vapor is always in the air, but it is invisible. You can see water vapor when you breathe out on a cold day. It looks like a little cloud when you breathe. You make a "cloud" in your bathroom when you take a hot shower on a cold day.

Observe the clouds in the sky where you live for a whole week.
    Are there clouds every day?
    Can you tell if the clouds have a lot of water drops?
    Did you have any rainy days? What did the clouds look like before it started to rain?
    Did you have any foggy days? How does it feel to walk in a "cloud"?

Have older students write a paragraph telling what they know about how a cloud is formed. Let them illustrate their paragraph in some way.

         How to Plan Your School Year

Weather Experiments and Activities

Prove that moving air can do work.

    1. Make a pinwheel.

    2. Make wind socks.

    3. Do a sailboat experiment.

Prove that there is water in the air.

    1. Water from the Air — Condensation

    2. Evaporation

       How does a cloud form?

Explore rainbows.

    1. Use a prism to show how light is broken up into its colors.

    2. Experiment with mixing the colors of the rainbow using food coloring or gelatin.

    3. Paint rainbows.

Create a ''weather station'' containing a wind sock, rain gauge, thermometer, and a weather vane. Record the weather outside your classroom window for an extended period of time.

Read weather maps and reports in the newspaper. Track the accuracy of the weather reports in your area.

Check an almanac for weather statistics. These statistics can be used to create ''search'' questions for older students.

Discuss myths about the weather.(For example: groundhog, Persephone)

            How to Plan Your School Year

April Showers
Bring May Flowers

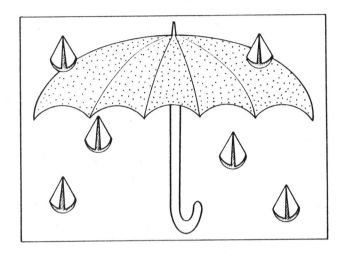

Watch the raindrops turn into flowers as if by magic! Fun for individuals to create or as a class bulletin board project.

Materials:

Construction paper
    white 12" X 18" (background)
    red 6" X 18" (umbrella)
      blue 4" square (raindrop/flower)
Chalk
Hair spray (to adhere chalk)
Black felt pen
Scissors
Glue

Steps to follow:

1. Cut the umbrella top from red paper.

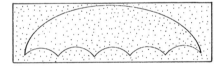

2. Paste the umbrella top to the background sheet.

   Use black felt pen to outline the umbrella, make the handle, and add curving ribs.

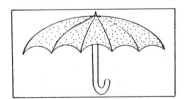

3. Fold the blue paper squares and trim.

4. Open the raindrops and create bright flowers inside using colored chalk.

   Spray the flowers lightly with hair spray to reduce smearing of the chalk.

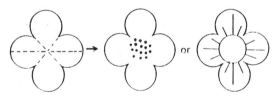

5. Fold the raindrops back up to hide the flowers and paste them to the background. Make as many raindrops as you wish.

   You and your friends can peek at the surprise flowers inside. It gives new meaning to the old saying "April showers bring May flowers."

Variations

Easter Time

Easter offers the perfect opportunity to combine the study of real rabbits, those in fiction, and Easter rabbits. Start by reading a good book.

Read about rabbits:

The Wild Rabbits; G. P. Putnam's Sons, 1980
Biography of a Cottontail by Lucille Trost; G. P. Putnam's Sons, 1971
The April Rabbits by David Cleveland; Coward, McCann & Gioghegan, 1978
Rabbit's Morning by Nancy Tafuri; Greenwillow, 1985
The Tale of Peter Rabbit by Beatrix Potter; Warne, 1902
The Country Bunny and the Little Gold Shoes by DuBose Heyward; Houghton, 1939
The Easter Bunny that Overslept by Otto & Priscilla Friedrich; Lothrop, 1983
Humbug Rabbit by Lorna Balian; Abingdon Press, 1974
Who's in the Egg? by A. & M. Provensen; Golden Press,
The Golden Egg Book by Margaret Wise Brown; Golden Press, 1947/1982

Think About It

Why are eggs a symbol of Easter?

Which countries/cultures celebrate Easter?

How did a rabbit become the deliverer of Easter eggs?

Rabbits and Hares

Rabbits and hares live all over the world. Some are large. Some are small. They come in many different colors and patterns. Most wild rabbits are brown. Brown rabbits have fur that turns white in the winter so they can hide in the snow.

Rabbits have short legs and move in little hops. Hares have strong, long back legs and can make big jumps. Rabbit babies are helpless when they are born. They cannot see and do not have fur. Hare babies have their eyes open and are covered with fur. They can hop soon after they are born.

Most rabbits live under the ground in tunnels called warrens. The mother rabbits build their nests in the warren. It is a safe place to hide from danger. Hares live above the ground. They dig little places to rest called forms. The mother hares build their nests up on the ground. In North America the cottontail rabbits live above the ground also.

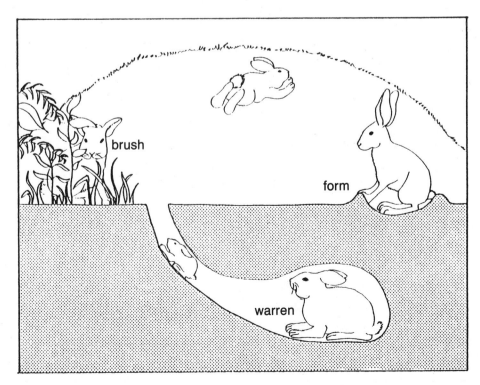

Activities About Real Rabbits and Hares

- Share books about rabbits and hares with your students. Discuss the characteristics that all mammals share. List the characteristics that are specific to rabbits and hares.

- Compare and contrast a rabbit and a hare. This may be done orally or as a writing assignment.

- Sequence the steps in the life cycle of a cottontail rabbit. Young students can use pictures (see page 55); children who have begun to write can combine pictures and sentences; older students can write a brief paragraph about each stage in the development of a rabbit or hare.

- Have each student bring in a rabbit to share with the class. These could be real (set specific guidelines about cages and care), stuffed, or pictures of various types of rabbits. Use the rabbits to develop vocabulary, compare and contrast characteristics, and as a starting point for creative writing.

- Write descriptive paragraphs about rabbits. Brainstorm before writing to help students have a rich source of ideas and vocabulary to work with.

- Draw rabbits. If your students are hesitant to try on their own, guide them through these steps. When they are finished drawing the rabbit, have them create an interesting background.

Cottontail Rabbits

A cottontail rabbit is small with brown fur and a fluffy white tail. It lives in the thick brush between the woods and fields. Strong back legs help the rabbit to run fast. Both hind feet hit the ground at the same time. The rabbit's long ears turn to pick up sounds. Sharp front teeth help rabbits eat plants.

The cottontail mother makes a nest of grass and bits of fur that she pulls from her belly. Baby cottontail rabbits are born alive. They are helpless. They do not have fur, their eyes are shut, and they cannot hear. Mother rabbit feeds the babies milk from her body.

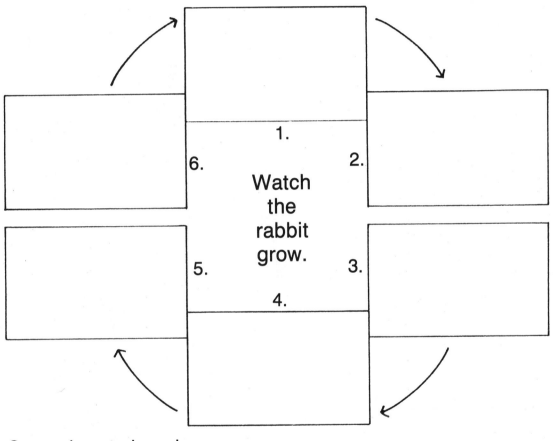

1.

6.

Watch
the
rabbit
grow.

2.

5.

3.

4.

Cut and paste in order:

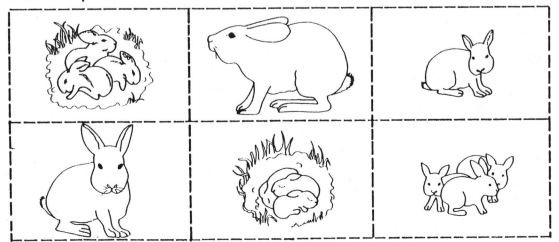

Draw imaginary rabbits using these ideas as a starting point. Older children may also write adventures for the characters.

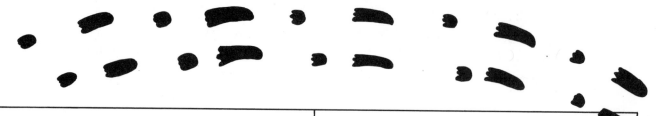

Horace Hare

Not all rabbits are soft and cuddly. Horace Hare has a terrible disposition. He can't get along with any of the other animals and is always up to mischief.

Get a sheet of paper and draw this evil-tempered hare. Let your picture show what kind of mischief Horace gets into.

Jake Jack Rabbit

Jake has had a miserable day. First he was chased by a hungry fox, then he fell into a muddy puddle while trying to escape.

Get a sheet of paper and draw Jake after his mishap. You may want to include the hungry fox in your picture.

Big Bad Bart Bunny

Bart's parents were very surprised when their cute, little bundle of fur continued to grow, and grow, and grow until he reached 6 feet 4 inches and 250 pounds. Today he supports his huge appetite by wrestling professionally.

Get a sheet of paper and draw Big Bad Bart in his championship bout.

Lillie Lop-Ears

Lillie was always a very lovely rabbit. Her silky ears fell down in the charming way of lop-ears, her little pink nose wiggled delightfully, while her dark eyes sparkled like twinkling stars. Lillie has become the star of T. V. and movies. This week her picture was on the cover of "Today in T. V." magazine.

Get a sheet of paper and draw lovely Lillie on the magazine cover.

A Book Project

The Tale of Peter Rabbit

Beatrix Potter; Warne, 1902

1. Read the story aloud to your students. Have them retell the story. Write each step on a sentence strip. Pass the strips out and have the children put them in the correct sequence. You may want to challenge older students (in pairs or groups of four) to rewrite the story in their own words.

2. Think About It — Ask questions such as these:
   "Can you tell which parts of this story are fiction and which parts could be true?"
   "Do you think Peter was a bad little rabbit? Why or why not?"
   "Do you have certain rules in your family about where you can and cannot go? Have you ever broken these rules? What happened?"
   "Why are rules sometimes necessary?"

3. Writing Activities — Select an activity appropriate to the age and ability of your students.
   Write a description of Peter. Include his physical appearance and his character.
   Write a new adventure for Peter. Decide where he will go and what happens to him when he gets there. Will he lose his jacket again?
   Create a story about a time when Peter does what his mother says and his three sisters are the ones who get into mischief.

4. Through the Gate — Make a gate "flap" that opens to show Peter. This can be simply an art activity or can become the cover for your students' original stories about Peter.

Draw a gate on construction paper.
Cut out the gate.
Make a fold along the left side.

Finish the picture.
Draw the fence and a picture of Peter.

A Book Project
An Egg is for Wishing
Helen Kay; Abelard-Schuman, 1966

reindeer—wealth

1. Read the story to your class. See if they can retell the story in the correct sequence.

2. Think About It — Ask questions such as these:

   "Why would someone be afraid of chickens?"

   "What did all of the animals in this story have in common?"

   "Can you think of any other animals that hatch from eggs?"

flower—love

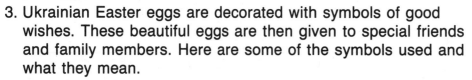

pine tree—love

3. Ukrainian Easter eggs are decorated with symbols of good wishes. These beautiful eggs are then given to special friends and family members. Here are some of the symbols used and what they mean.

   Give each child a large egg shape cut from colored construction paper. Decorate this egg with an "Easter wish." Give the egg to a special friend.

4. Have your students make up their own "picture languages." Let them write messages using their pictures. See if they can read each others' messages.

hen and rooster—wishes coming true

spiral—growing

A Book Project
The Country Bunny and the Little Gold Shoes
DuBose Heyward; Houghton, 1939

1. Read the story. Guide students to recall the important events in the story.

2. Think About It — Ask questions such as these:

   "Is this story fact or fiction? How can you tell?"

   "Can the Easter bunny be female? Why or why not?"

   "How would you describe the character of the little country bunny?"

3. Writing Activities — Select an activity appropriate to the age and ability of your students.

   Write about the part of the story that you liked the best.

   Pretend you had to deliver all of those eggs. You don't have magic golden shoes. What could you use to help?

   Challenge your students to write an application for the position of substitute Easter bunny. Explain that they will need to explain what qualities and experiences they possess that would make them good candidates for the job.

How to Plan Your School Year

Note: This activity is from EMC 207 *How to Make Books With Children.*

A Bunny Book

Any of the writing experiences about rabbits and hares can be put into this charming book cover.

Steps:

1. Front Cover
   Round the corners of a white tagboard rectangle.
   Glue on a piece of pink paper.

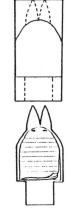

2. Back Cover
   Lay the front cover on a larger sheet of tagboard. Sketch around it and add the ears and feet. Cut on these lines.
   Staple the finished stories to the back cover. Staple only across the top.

3. Hinge the front cover across the top. Attach the front cover with two paper fasteners. These are also eyes for the bunny.
   Add details with felt pens: fuzzy feet, pink ears, arms, pink nose.
   Curl the ears forward.
   Print the title.

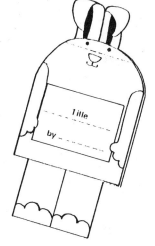

Creative Writing Ideas

• Story Starters

On Easter morning, Stella looked into her basket and discovered...

Arturo woke up Easter morning to find he had turned into a...

I don't want the Easter Bunny to get lost, so I am sending directions (or a map that shows) how to get to my house.

How many different ways can you think of to color Easter eggs? Tell how you would do each one.

I have never seen such a huge Easter egg before. It has a crack up the side. What could be trying to hatch out?

Easter morning at my house ...

• Titles for Easter Stories

The First Easter Rabbit

The Egg Factory

The Easter Rabbit Training Manual

A Really Strange Egg Hunt

Easter Art

• Make a cross-legged bunny to sit on the corner of your desk.

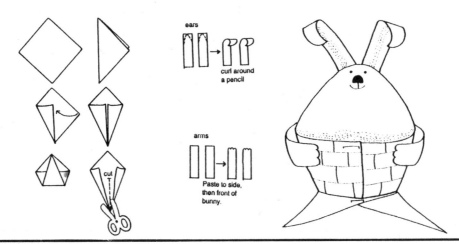

• Make a chain of festive bunnies to decorate a bulletin board.

• Make bunny ears from a brown lunch bag.

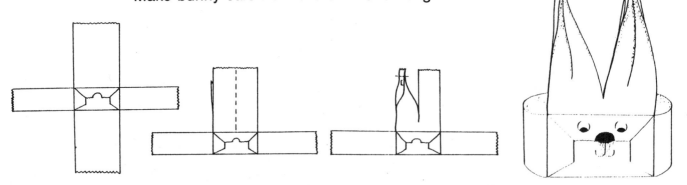

• Make bunny "bags" and bunny "boxes" instead of baskets this year.

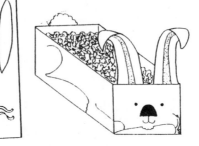

Activities for May

Other celebrations to plan this month:

May 1 - Mother Goose Day
May 5 - Children's Day in Japan
May 22 - International Frog Jumping Contest
Shoe Week/Foot Health Month
National Bicycle Month
National Photo Month

Authors' May Birthdays:

May 1 - Charles Shaw	*It Looked Like Spilt Milk*
May 4 - Don Wood	*The Napping House*
May 5 - Leo Lionni	*Frederick*
May 12 - Caroline Feller Bauer	*Too Many Books*
May 22 - Arnold Lobel	*The Book of Pigericks*
May 25 - Ivy Ruckman	*Night of the Twisters*

         How to Plan Your School Year

Special May Celebrations

National Pickle Week

Sample all the various kinds of pickles available in your grocery store. Create a graph to determine which was liked the best or the least.

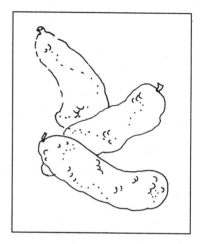

Give each child a large piece of green construction paper and have them make Pickle Personalities. They can then write about their pickle. Is it a Gherkin, Sweet, Dill...? What kind of adventures will they have?

> *Pickle Things* by Marc Brown
> *Pickle, Pickle, Pickle Juice* by Patty Wolcott

Read the book *Pickle Things* by Marc Brown and have children rewrite it, telling their own version using strange and unusual fruits and vegetables.

How Does Your Garden Grow?

April flowers bring May flowers and fruits and vegetables and the question... How Does Your Garden Grow? Have your older students design a garden. Bring in seed catalogs and incorporate math by having them calculate the cost. If you are fortunate enough to have the space, go ahead and plant a real garden.

Create alphabet books using fruits and vegetables or flowers as a theme. These are challenging for students of all ages.

> *Growing Vegetable Soup* by Lois Ehlert
> *Planting a Rainbow* By Lois Ehlert

May Day

May Day is honored all over the world! The Romans celebrated it originally as a welcome to spring. In the Middle Ages, people in Europe celebrated the day by dancing around a May pole. Share with your class the old custom of leaving a basket full of flowers on a friend's doorstep. as a surprise on the first day of May.

Make May Baskets

Each child will need a 9" X 12" sheet of colored construction paper to make this May basket.

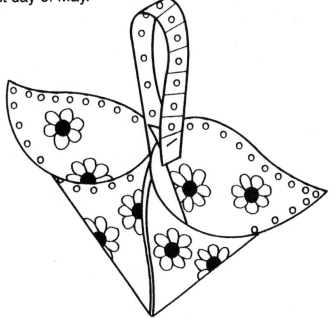

1. Cut a 3" piece off the construction paper. Save the smaller piece for a handle.

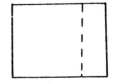

2. Fold the square into quarters.

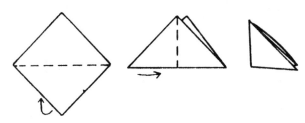

3. Open the folded paper. Use crayons to color bright flowers all over both sides of the square. OPTIONAL: Use a hole punch around the edge for a lacy look.

4. Place an index finger in the center and press down firmly. Pull up the two corners that border the fold. Cross over the ends and staple.

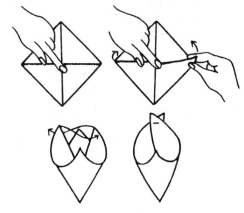

5. Fold the handle piece.

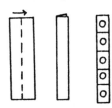

Fold the handle over the stapled basket ends. Staple again through all layers.

The May Basket

The first day of May is a time for spring surprises. One nice surprise is the giving of a May basket to someone you like. It is easy to do. First, you need a basket. You can make one from folded paper or by covering a can or box with pretty paper. Don't forget to make a handle.

Next you will need to fill the basket with spring flowers. Be sure you ask permission before you pick them.

Now comes a very important step. You must decide to whom you will give the basket. Have you made up your mind? Good. You are ready for the best part.

Sneak up to the person's front door. Be sure that no one sees you. Sit the basket on the front step, or hang it on the doorknob. Ring the bell, or knock on the door. When you hear someone coming, run quickly and hide where you can see your friend find the surprise basket. Maybe someone you know will leave a May basket on your doorstep. Wouldn't that be fun?

Think About It:

How many different ways to make a basket can you think of?

Cinco de Mayo

Cinco de Mayo
Is a special date
That Mexicans
Choose to celebrate.

Leslie Tryon

Cinco de Mayo commemorates the victory by the Mexican army over invading French forces at Pueblo, Mexico in 1862. On the fifth of May, many Americans of Mexican descent celebrate the occasion with fiestas and friends.

Piñatas and Paper Flowers: Holidays of the Americas in English and Spanish by Lila Perl; Houghton Mifflin, 1983
Fiesta by June Behrens; Childrens Press, 1976
Mexico by Karen Jacobsen; Childrens Press, 1983
A Family in Mexico by Peter Jacobsen; Watts, 1984
Family Pictures by Carmen Lomas Garza; Children's Book Press, 1990

Think About It

There are people from many different countries and cultures in the United States of America. Can you think of ways in which each group is the same? In what ways are they different?

In what ways has the culture of Mexico affected the U.S.A.?

Brainstorm to create a list of all the Spanish words you can think of that have become part of the English language.

Activities

• Locate Mexico and France on a world map or globe.
• Count the number of children in class who are from Mexico or who had ancestors who came from Mexico. Tally how many celebrate Cinco de Mayo. Discuss what occurs in their homes on that day.
• Plan a celebration. Decorate the room with bright colors. Plan appropriate music, treats, and activities.

Mother's Day

Read some of these delightful books about mothers and children.

The Terrible Thing that Happened at Our House by Marge Blaine; Four Winds Press, 1975
I Wish Laura's Mommy was My Mommy by Barbara Power; Lippencott, 1979
Mother's Mother's Day by Lorna Balian; Abingdon, 1982
On Mother's Lap by Ann Herbert Scott; McGraw-Hill, 1972
Martha Ann and the Mother Store by Nathaniel and Betty Jo Carnley; Harcourt Brace Jovanovich, 1973
Mother, Mother, I want another by Maria Plushkin; Crown, 1976
The Mother's Day Mice by Eve Bunting; Clarion Books, 1986
My Mom Travels a Lot by Caroline Feller Bauer; Puffin, 1981
A Chair for My Mother by Vera B. Williams; Greenwillow, 1982
Ramona and her Mother by Beverly Cleary; Dell, 1979

Mother's Day Activities

- Mother Reports

  Have children interview their mothers (or a grandmother, aunt, or other female caretaker) to find out information they don't know. You may want to assign only one part to younger students.

  ### Part 1 : A Description

  Write a paragraph telling what she looks like. Make it clear and complete.

  ### Part 2: Her Childhood

  Write one or two paragraphs about when she was a girl. Include when and where she was born, what it was like where she lived growing up, her likes and dislikes, and any other interesting information about that time in her life.

  ### Part 3: As an Adult

  Write one or more paragraphs about her now. Include her job, her special interests and talents, and what she likes and dislikes now.

  ### Part 4: Is she special?

  Include a picture of mother as a child and as an adult.

- Make a special greeting card. For example:

  A Trainload of Wishes for Mom

A Trainload of Wishes for Mom

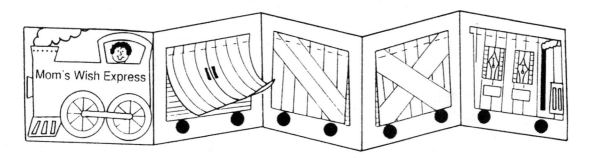

Materials:

- Accordion–folded paper for the basic card form. Each segment is 5" X 6". Choose from:
  1. Construction paper, folded and taped on fold line
  2. Butcher paper double-folded for strength
  3. Tagboard, cut and taped on folds.
- Each child will need a copy of the patterns on the following page

- 3½" X 5" construction paper flaps for train cars (3 per train)
- 3½" X 5" sheets of writing paper for under flaps (4 per train)
- Black construction paper 1" squares for wheels (8 per train)
- Felt pens, scissors and paste

Steps to follow:

1. Assemble the accordion–folded basic card shape.

2. Color and cut out the engine and caboose forms. Each child draws himself/herself in the engineer's seat (or paste a small picture).

3. Decorate 3 train car flaps. Fold down the top edge.

4. Round the corners of the black squares to form wheels.

5. Paste:
   a. Engine on the first segment. Add smoke coming out of the smokestack.

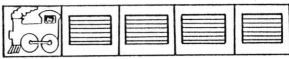

b. Writing paper to the next four segments.
c. Paste wheels below each writing paper.
d. Paste "car" flaps over the three train cars. (Paste along the folded flap.)
e. Paste the caboose flap on the last segment.

6. Draw couplings between each of the cars.

7. Write a wish for Mom under each flap. Sign your name under the caboose.

Patterns for Mom's Trainload of Wishes

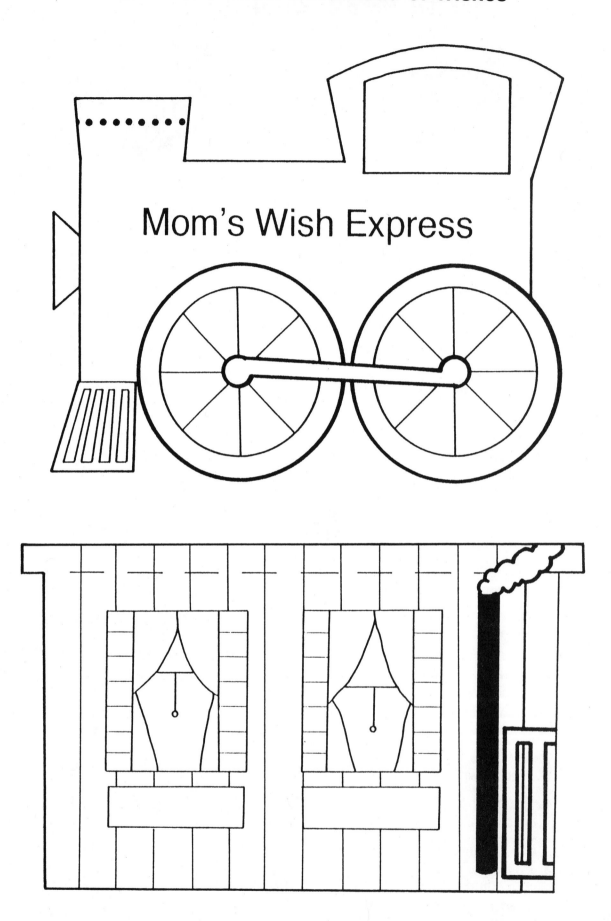

Mom's Wish Express

Celebrate Summer

Facts about summer:

• The approximate months of summer are June, July and August.

• Summer Solstice - June 21
The sun is as far north as it gets, causing this day to be the longest of the year.

• During these months, the North Pole is tilted towards the sun causing warmer and longer days because of the more direct sun rays.

• Some animals go dormant during the summer. This is called "estivation."

• High temperatures and low moisture can cause fire danger.

     How to Plan Your School Year

Poems for Summer

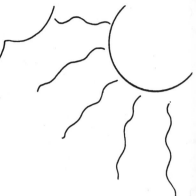

Summer

In August, when the days are hot,
I like to find a shady spot,
And hardly move a single bit-
And sit-
     And sit-
          And sit.

Anonymous

Sunshine

Have you ever see the sun shine,
the sun shine,
the sun shine,
Have you ever seen the sun shine
On a hot summer's day?

It gives light and warms you.
It helps trees and flowers too.

Have you ever seen the sun shine
On a hot summer's day?

Jo Ellen Moore

Our Sun

A ball of burning gases
Shines brightly down
Lighting our day-time hours
As the earth turns 'round.

It is that glowing star
We call the sun,
Far-off in the sky, yet
Warming everyone.

Jo Ellen Moore

 How to Plan Your School Year

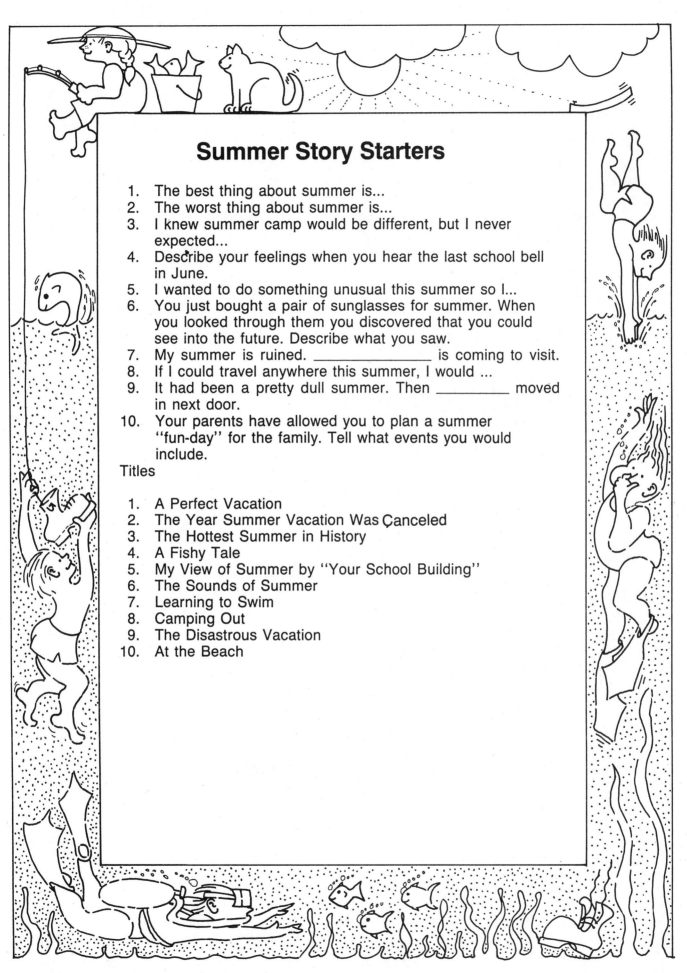

Summer Story Starters

1. The best thing about summer is...
2. The worst thing about summer is...
3. I knew summer camp would be different, but I never expected...
4. Describe your feelings when you hear the last school bell in June.
5. I wanted to do something unusual this summer so I...
6. You just bought a pair of sunglasses for summer. When you looked through them you discovered that you could see into the future. Describe what you saw.
7. My summer is ruined. _____ is coming to visit.
8. If I could travel anywhere this summer, I would ...
9. It had been a pretty dull summer. Then _____ moved in next door.
10. Your parents have allowed you to plan a summer "fun-day" for the family. Tell what events you would include.

Titles

1. A Perfect Vacation
2. The Year Summer Vacation Was Canceled
3. The Hottest Summer in History
4. A Fishy Tale
5. My View of Summer by "Your School Building"
6. The Sounds of Summer
7. Learning to Swim
8. Camping Out
9. The Disastrous Vacation
10. At the Beach

Activities for June

Other celebrations to plan this month:

1st Monday - National Spelling Bee
Smile Day
Zoo Month

Authors' June Birthdays:

June 6 - Cynthia Rylant	*The Relatives Came*
June 10 - Maurice Sendak	*Where the Wild Things Are*
June 12 - Helen Lester	*Tacky the Penguin*
June 18 - Chris Van Allsburg	*Jumanji*
June 25 - Eric Carle	*The Very Hungry Caterpillar*
June 30 - David McPhail	*Pig Pig Grows Up*

Special June Celebrations

U.S. Flag Day

Discuss the design of our flag. The thirteen stripes represent the original thirteen states. There is a star for each of the fifty states. Sing "The Star Spangled Banner" and discuss the meaning of the vocabulary in the *Pledge of Allegieance*.

> *Stars and Stripes* by Mae Blacker Freeman; Random House
> *The Star Spangled Banner* by Peter Spier; Doubleday

Dairy Month

Celebrate National Dairy Month with a variety of activities. Brainstorm with your children to list all of the things we use that come from milk. Have a cheese tasting day. Do all cheeses come from cow's milk? Make butter. All you need is a medium-sized jar with a tight-fitting lid and whipping cream. Have children take turns shaking the cream. When it's done add a little salt and eat on crackers.

Now move on to greater things and make ice cream in your class. (Choose a recipe suitable for the freezer you are using.) Share Shel Silverstein's poem "Eighteen Flavors" as you eat your own creation. Make a giant cone and have each child make a "dip" of ice cream for a display to go with a delightful poem.

> *From Milk to Ice Cream* by Ali Mitgutsch
> *Donna O'Neeshuck was Chased by Some Cows* by Bill Grossman
> *The Milk Makers* by Gail Gibbons
> *From Cow to Carton* by Gail Gibbons

Aquarium Month

Let's study the wonderful varieties of fish and invertebrates that live in aquariums. It offers vocabulary development, science investigation and opportunities to stimulate student nonfiction writing.

> *Fishes* by Brian Wildsmith
> *A Fishy Color Story* by Joanne and David Wylie
> *Sea Squares* by Joy N. Hulme
> *A House for Hermit Crab* by Eric Carle

Note: Practice creating acrostics as a group using summer-related words before requiring children to do this independently.

In the Good Old Summertime

Swimming

Until

My

Mom

Expects me to

Return

Summer means sitting

Under my favorite

Monkey Puzzle tree each

Morning until

Exactly 10:00 when

Richard comes to play

Write one word or phrase that begins with each letter of the word SUMMER. Your finished poem must complete a thought about summertime.

S _____

U _____

M _____

M _____

E _____

R _____

How to Plan Your School Year

Prints from Nature

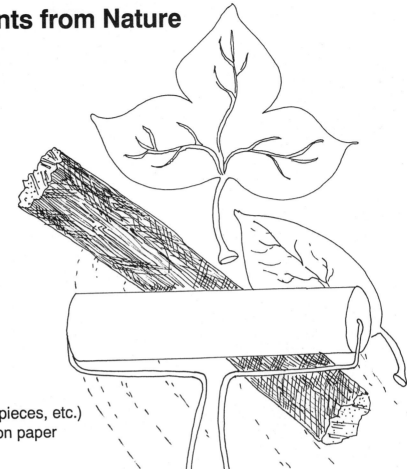

With a little practice, children can create beautiful works of art using items they find in nature. You may want to take a quick walking "field trip" around the neighborhood to collect items to use in this activity. If you do fish prints, be sure to keep the fish on ice when not being used. The materials list recommends construction paper. If your budget is tight, use brown paper bags and newspapers for practice or for the final print. The results may surprise you.

Materials:
• items from nature (fish, shells, wood pieces, etc.)
• 12" x 18" (30.5 x 45.7 cm) construction paper
  in a variety of colors
• tempera paint
• brayer and large plate
• felt pens
• paper towels

Steps to follow:
1. Go on a nature walk or bring from home a collection of items that have an interesting textured surface that is fairly flat. Be sure the surface of the item used for the printing is dry and clean to start with.

2. Offer students a selection of paint and paper that are contrasting colors...black paper and white paint, blue paint and yellow paper, etc.

3. Put a small amount of paint on a large plate.
Roll the brayer in the paint until it is completely coated.

4. Roll the brayer over the textured area of one of the items.

5. Press the paint-covered area onto the construction paper.
Repeat as many times as desired to create an interesting design.

6. Your students may wish to carry the project one step farther and add details with felt tip pens.

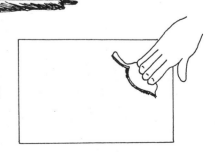

Sandcasting

This activity is the most fun if done at the beach, of course! However, a sandbox or a plastic tub full of sand works just as well. This can be messy so smocks and a well-covered floor are a good idea.

Materials:

- sand
- large plastic tub
- plaster of Paris
- small shells, pebbles, driftwood
- spoons
- bucket or can for mixing plaster of Paris
- water
- clean stiff paint brush
- large paper clips (optional)
- water

Steps to follow:

1. Moisten the sand (damp, not wet). Using hands and spoons, form a design in the sand. Don't make it too deep or too large, otherwise it will take forever to dry.   A couple of inches (5 cm) deep and six inches (15 cm) or so wide is a nice size. Simple shapes such as a starfish, scallop shell, sun, or fish work best.

2. Add details by drawing in the sand. You may also place shells, pebbles and/or bits of driftwood in the hole to form part of your design.

3. Mix plaster of Paris according to the directions on the package. Pour the liquid plaster into the hole, filling it just to the surface. Let the sandcasting dry undisturbed. The drying time will depend on how large a sandcasting has been made.

If you wish to hang the sandcastings, add a large paper clip "hook" when the sandcasting has set somewhat, but before it has dried completely.

4. Lift the dry sandcasting carefully from the sand. Brush off the excess sand and admire your wonderful creation!

 How to Plan Your School Year

Here Comes the Sun

What would summer be if we couldn't count on sunny days to enjoy all the fun activities requiring sunshine. Transform your classroom into the "brightest" spot in school for a few weeks with these "hot" activities.

Sun Mobiles

Materials:

- white paper plates (one per child)
- pieces of sponge
- yellow, orange, and red tempera paint
- flat tins for paint
- paper in a variety of warm colors
- string or yarn

How to Make:

1. Sponge paint one side of the paper plate. Encourage children to use one color, let it dry, then add another.

2. Cut sun "rays" using the template. Children may want to use one color or several colors.

3. Glue the rays to the outside edge of the "sun."

4. Punch a hole in the top edge, tie string or yarn through the hole, and hang.

   Variation: Before adding the rays to the sun, have the children write something they learned during the year on each ray. Use black felt tip pen so the words can be seen.

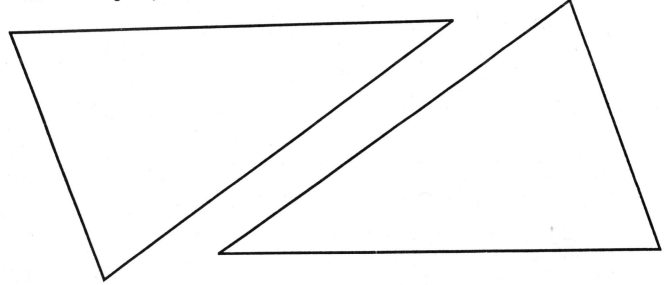

Father's Day

Read some of these books about fathers.

Daddy Makes the Best Spaghetti by Anna Grossnickle Hines; Clarion Books, 1986
Ten, Nine, Eight by Molly Bang; Puffin, 1983
Ramona and her Father by Beverly Cleary; Dell, 1977
Like Jake and Me by Mavis Jukes; Knopf, 1984
Daddy is a Monster...Sometimes by John Steptoe; Harper 1980
A Father Like That by Charlotte Zolotow; Harper, 1966
My Dad Takes Care of Me by P. Quinlan; Annick Press, 1987

Father's Day Activities

• Father Reports
   Have children interview their fathers (grandfather, uncle, or other male caretaker) and write reports following the guidelines set up for Mother reports.

• Visiting Day
   Invite fathers (or mothers for Mother's Day) to visit class. They may tell about their occupations, share a special skill, or simply enjoy seeing how their children spend a day at school. You may want to do one of the following also.
      Have your students practice how to make an introduction.
      Prepare a special treat to eat at break time.
      Practice poems, songs, or original playlets to perform for the fathers (mothers).

• Make a special greeting card. For example:

A Shirt and Tie for Father's Day

A Shirt and Tie for Father's Day

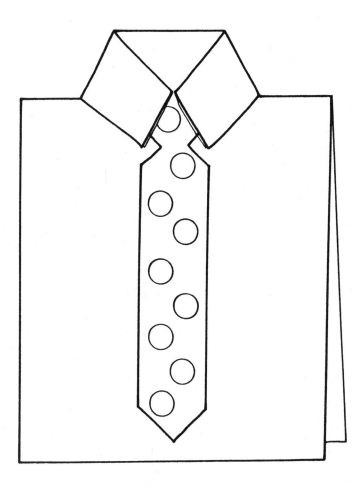

This simple shirt and tie open to become a clever greeting card for Dad's special day.

Materials:
Construction paper
    white 4½'' X 11'' (shirt)
    various colors 1¼'' X 4'' (tie)
Ruler
Pencil
Scissors
Paste

Steps to follow:

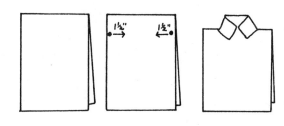

1. Fold the white paper in half to form the shirt.
   Measure down 1'' from the fold. Make a dot. Draw a 1½'' line in from the dot. (Do this on both edges of the paper.)
   Cut on the lines you drew.
2. Fold in at an angle to form the collar.
3. Cut a tie from the colored strip.
4. Paste the tie to the shirt.
5. Open the shirt and write a special Father's Day message for your dad.

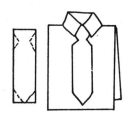

Activities for July

Other celebrations to plan this month:

July 1 - Canada Day
July 3 - (and Aug 14) - Dog Days of Summer
July 7 - Star Festival - Poems on Bamboo Branches
Week of the 20th - Space Week
Anti-Boredom Month
National Ice Cream Month
National Hot Dog Month

Authors' July Birthdays:

July 11 - Patricia Polacco   *Thundercake*
July 14 - Laura Joffe Numeroff   *If You Give a Mouse a Cookie*
July 14 - Peggy Parrish   *Amelia Bedelia*
July 25 - Ron Barrett   *Cloudy with a Chance of Meatballs*
July 28 - Beatrix Potter   *The Tale of Peter Rabbit*

Picnic Month

Pack a picnic and head off for your favorite picnic spot. What will you take? Who will you bring? What will you do at the picnic besides eat? What will you do to keep the ants away? Real or imaginary, picnics are great fun and full of learning possibilities.

• Make a pop-up book showing what is inside your picnic basket.

• Write a class story about all of the little uninvited guests that often show up at picnics.

• Set up a center with a red checkered cloth and display your supply of summer reading books inside a picnic basket.

Space Month

Blast off for the whole month of July and soar through the solar system. Research planets, use math skills to calculate how long it will take you to get where you are going at different speeds. Discover which planet is the most like our own.

Exploring the Night Sky by Terence Dickinson
Sun Up, Sun Down by Gail Gibbons
The Moon Seems to Change by Franklyn M. Branley
The Nightgown of the Sullen Moon by Nancy Willard

Independence Day Story Starters

1. You have designed a float for the Independence Day parade. Describe it in detail.
2. My parents had said no firecrackers, but Joe had some, so ...
3. Last July Fourth I entered the pie-eating contest on a dare.
4. What a disaster! Mom let my older sister Jody and her friend Tamara make our picnic lunch.
5. Why do you think people celebrate Independence Day?

Titles

1. How to Plan a Fourth of July Picnic
2. Fireworks Safety
3. Independence Day
4. How My Family Celebrates July Fourth
5. How Fireworks Were Invented

Independence Day - U.S.A.
A Crossword Puzzle

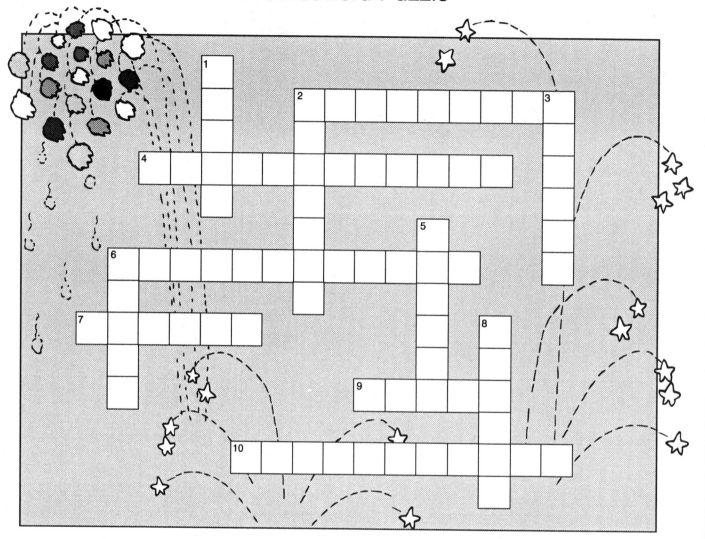

ACROSS
2. explosive devices for making a display of bright lights and loud noises high in the sky
4. freedom from control by others
6. _____ is Independence Day in the U.S.A.
7. a public procession usually having marching bands and floats
9. sounds organized to have rhythm, melody and harmony
10. festive activities for a special occasion

DOWN
1. marching _____ are musical groups in a parade
2. the power to determine your own actions without asking the permission of others
3. a form of communication spoken before an audience
5. vehicles carrying displays in a parade are called
6. pieces of cloth containing special colors or symbols to represent nations
8. we took our lunch to the park in a _____ basket

How to Plan Your School Year

Explosion in the Fireworks Factory

Willie went to bed at his usual time, but he couldn't sleep. He was too excited about tomorrow's celebrations. Independence Day meant a parade, speeches, music, great food and best of all, fireworks!

Suddenly Willie heard sirens and people yelling. He ran to the window and looked out. The sky was filled with flashing lights and bright colors. Matt's Fireworks Plant had exploded!

Write...
   a paragraph describing how the sky looked
   a story explaining what caused the explosion
   a news report about the big disaster

Create...
   a drawing or painting of the explosion
   a torn paper collage of the colors in the explosion
   an etching of fireworks in the night sky

Bonus: Find out if fireworks are allowed in your community. If they are, make a list of rules for fireworks safety. Share your list with your classmates.

Fireworks Light Up the Sky

Fireworks are always exciting. Watching the flashes of color exploding across the sky, then sparkling "stars" drifting down toward the earth has to elicit "ooh"s and "ah"s. Challenge your students to recreate these exciting explosions of color in the activity below.

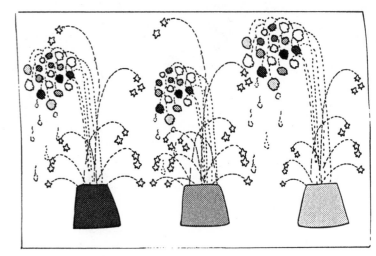

Materials:
• 12" x 18" (30.5 x 45.7 cm) sheet of dark blue construction paper
• 3" (7.5 cm) squares of construction paper in bright colors: red, yellow, pink, and green
• saucers with different colors of tempera paint: red, white, pink, and yellow
• one saucer with a puddle of white glue
• glitter
• small printing tools: pencil erasers, fingers, Q -Tips or sponge pieces
• paste

Steps to follow:

1. Set up a printing center. Arrange for two or three students to work at a time.

2. The class may begin this experiment by working at their individual desks with paper and paste. Give each student three squares of paper, one each of three different colors. Students trim the sides to create a cone shape and then they use the scraps to decorate the cones. Students paste the decorated cones to the bottom of their large blue construction paper.

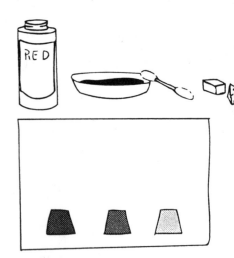

3. At this point, students take turns going to the print center to add colorful fireworks to their picture. They need to experiment with several different techniques using the pencil erasers, fingers, etc., on newsprint before they do the actual printing on the blue construction paper. It is interesting to use both paint and sprinkled glitter on dots of glue.

Encourage students to experiment with different techniques.

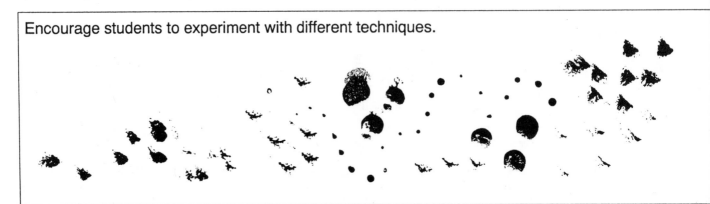

Note: Brainstorm all the types of activities, exciting and disastrous, that might happen at summer camp. Give children a copy of this form and set their imaginations to work as they practice writing friendly letters.

News from Camp

_____

_____

_____

_____

_____

_____

_____

_____

_____

_____

_____

_____

_____

Activities for August

Other celebrations to plan this month:

August 13 - International Left-hander's Day
Olympics
National Smile Week

Authors' August Birthdays:

August 1 - Bill Wallace	*Trapped in Death Cave*
August 1 - Gail Gibbons	*From Cow to Carton*
August 6 - Barbara Cooney	*Miss Rumphius*
August 11 - Joanna Cole	*The Magic School Bus*
August 12 - Mary Ann Hoberman	*A House is a House for Me*
August 30 - Donald Crews	*Freight Train*